Programming in Java

Programming in JAVA

Preeti Jain

CENTRUM PRESS
NEW DELHI-110002 (INDIA)

CENTRUM PRESS
H.O.: 4360/4, Ansari Road, Daryaganj,
New Delhi-110002 (India)
Tel: 23278000, 23261597, 23255577, 23286875
B.O.: No. 1015, Ist Main Road, BSK IIIrd Stage,
IIIrd Phase, IIIrd Block, Bangalore-560085 (INDIA)
Tel: 080-41723429
Email: centrumpress@gmail.com
Visit us at: www.centrumpress.com

Programming in Java

First Edition, 2011

PRINTED IN INDIA

Printed at Tarun Offset Printers, Delhi-110053

Contents

Preface

When Java appeared it is immediately noticed that its potential as a language for beginning programmers is really unique. Java satisfies today's need for early instruction in an object-oriented language, while avoiding the complexities of C++. At the same time, Java is similar enough to C++ to serve as a steppingstone to that language.

With no pointers to cause problems, Java programs are immune to those frustrating crashes that are so common in C++. If a Java program does encounter an error at run time, the interpreter provides a stack trace that can often pinpoint the problem. Last but not least, the software needed to write and execute Java programs can be downloaded from the Web at no charge.

Although GUI programming is an important part of developing software, it's not the central focus of this book. There's little point in subjecting beginners to the myriad of details that are required in developing professional GUI applications.

Author

1

Introduction

PROGRAMMING CONCEPT

The Java programming language is a general-purpose, concurrent, class-based, object-oriented language. It is designed to be simple enough that many programmers can achieve fluency in the language. The Java programming language is related to C and C++ but is organized rather differently, with a number of aspects of C and C++ omitted and a few ideas from other languages included. It is intended to be a production language, not a research language, and so, as C. A. R. Hoare suggested in his classic paper on language design, the design has avoided including new and untested features.

The Java programming language is strongly typed. This specification clearly distinguishes between the *compile-time errors* that can and must be detected at compile time, and those that occur at run time. Compile time normally consists of translating programs into a machine-independent byte code representation. Run-time activities include loading and linking of the classes needed to execute a program, optional machine code generation and dynamic optimization of the program, and actual program execution.

The Java programming language is a relatively high-level language, in that details of the machine representation are not available through the language. It includes automatic storage management, typically using a garbage collector, to avoid the safety problems of explicit deallocation (as in C's `free` or C++'s `delete`). High-performance garbage-collected implementations can have bounded pauses to support systems programming and real-time applications. The language does not include any unsafe constructs, such as array accesses without index checking, since such unsafe constructs would cause a program to behave in an unspecified way.

The Java programming language provides control over the scope of names and supports limitations on external access to members of packages, classes, and interfaces. This helps in writing large programs by distinguishing the implementation of a type from its users and those who extend it. Recommended naming conventions that make for more readable programs are described here.

Classes support single implementation inheritance, in which the implementation of each class is derived from that of a single superclass, and ultimately from the class `Object`. Variables of a class type can reference an instance of that class or of any subclass of that class, allowing new types to be used with existing methods, polymorphically.

Classes support concurrent programming with `synchronized` methods. Methods declare the checked exceptions that can arise from their execution, which allows compile-time checking to ensure that exceptional conditions are handled. Objects can declare a `finalize` method that will be invoked before the objects are discarded by the garbage collector, allowing the objects to clean up their state.

For simplicity, the language has neither declaration "headers" separate from the implementation of a class nor separate type and class hierarchies.

A special form of classes, enums, support the definition of small sets of values and their manipulation in a type safe manner. Unlike enumerations in other languages, enums are objects and may have their own methods.

After initialization, class methods and class variables may be used. Some classes may be instantiated to create new objects of the class type. Objects that are class instances also contain an instance of each superclass of the class, and object creation involves recursive creation of these superclass instances. When an object is no longer referenced, it may be reclaimed by the garbage collector. If an object declares a finalizer, the finalizer is executed before the object is reclaimed to give the object a last chance to clean up resources that would not otherwise be released. When a class is no longer needed, it may be unloaded.

EXAMPLE PROGRAMS

Most of the example programs given in the text are ready to be executed and are similar in form to:

```
class Test {
    public static void main(String[] args) {
        for (int i = 0; i < args.length; i++)
            System.out.print(i == 0 ? args[i]:
" " + args[i]);
        System.out.println();
    }
}
```

On a Sun workstation using Sun's Java 2 Platform Standard Edition Develpment Kit software, this class, stored in the file `Test.java`, can be compiled and executed by giving the commands:

```
javac Test.java
java Test Hello, world.
```

producing the output:

```
Hello, world.
```

NOTATION

Throughout this book we refer to classes and interfaces drawn from the Java and Java 2 platforms. Whenever we refer to a class or interface which is not defined in an example in this book using a single identifier N, the intended reference is to the class or interface named N in the package `java.lang`. We use the canonical name for classes or interfaces from packages other than `java.lang`.

RELATIONSHIP

As noted above, this specification often refers to classes of the Java and Java 2 platforms. In particular, some classes have a special relationship with the Java programming language.

Examples include classes such as `Object`, `Class`, `ClassLoader`, `String`, `Thread`, and the classes and interfaces in package `java.lang.reflect`, among others. The language definition constrains the behaviour of these classes and interfaces, but this document does not provide a complete specification for them. The reader is referred to other parts of the Java platform specification for such detailed API specifications.

Thus this document does not describe reflection in any detail. Many linguistic constructs have analogues in the reflection API, but these are generally not discussed here. So, for example, when we list the ways in which an object can be created, we generally do not include the ways in which the reflective API can accomplish this. Readers should be aware of these additional mechanisms even though they are not mentioned in this text.

CONTEXT-FREE GRAMMARS

A context-free grammar consists of a number of productions. Each production has an abstract symbol called a nonterminal as its left-hand side, and a sequence of one or more nonterminal and terminal symbols as its right-hand side. For each grammar, the terminal symbols are drawn from a specified *alphabet*.

Starting from a sentence consisting of a single distinguished nonterminal, called the goal symbol, a given context-free grammar specifies a language, namely, the set of possible sequences of terminal symbols that can result from repeatedly replacing any nonterminal in the sequence with a right-hand side of a production for which the nonterminal is the left-hand side.

THE LEXICAL GRAMMAR

A lexical grammar for the Java programming language is given in. This grammar has as its terminal symbols the characters of the Unicode character set. It defines a set of productions, starting from the goal symbol Input, that describe how sequences of Unicode characters are translated into a sequence of input elements. These input elements, with white space and comments discarded, form the terminal symbols for the syntactic grammar for the Java programming language and are called tokens. These tokens are the identifiers, keywords, literals, separators, and operators of the Java programming language.

THE SYNTACTIC GRAMMAR

This grammar has tokens defined by the lexical grammar as its terminal symbols. It defines a set of productions, starting from the goal symbol *CompilationUnit*, that describe how sequences of tokens can form syntactically correct programs.

GRAMMAR NOTATION

Terminal symbols are shown in **`fixed width`** font in the productions of the lexical and syntactic grammars, and throughout this specification whenever the text is directly referring to such a terminal symbol. These are to appear in a program exactly as written.

Nonterminal symbols are shown in *italic* type. The definition of a nonterminal is introduced by the name of the nonterminal being defined followed by a colon. One or more alternative right-hand sides for the nonterminal then follow on succeeding lines. For example, the syntactic definition:

```
IfThenStatement:
        if ( Expression ) Statement
```

states that the nonterminal *IfThenStatement* represents the token **`if`**, followed by a left parenthesis token, followed by an *Expression*, followed by a right parenthesis token, followed by a *Statement*.

As another example, the syntactic definition:

```
ArgumentList:
        Argument
        ArgumentList , Argument
```

states that an *ArgumentList* may represent either a single *Argument* or an *ArgumentList*, followed by a comma, followed by an *Argument*. This definition of *ArgumentList* is *recursive*, that is to say, it is defined in terms of itself. The result is that an

ArgumentList may contain any positive number of arguments. Such recursive definitions of nonterminals are common.

The subscripted suffix "opt", which may appear after a terminal or nonterminal, indicates an optional symbol. The alternative containing the optional symbol actually specifies two right-hand sides, one that omits the optional element and one that includes it.

This means that:

```
BreakStatement:
     break Identifieropt ;
```

is a convenient abbreviation for:

```
BreakStatement:
     break ;
     break Identifier ;
```

and that:

```
BasicForStatement:
     for ( ForInitopt ; Expressionopt ; ForUpdateopt ) Statement
```

is a convenient abbreviation for:

```
BasicForStatement:
for (; Expressionopt ; ForUpdateopt ) Statement
for ( ForInit ; Expressionopt ; ForUpdateopt ) Statement
```

which in turn is an abbreviation for:

```
BasicForStatement:
     for (; ; ForUpdateopt ) Statement
     for (; Expression ; ForUpdateopt ) Statement
     for ( ForInit ; ; ForUpdateopt ) Statement
     for ( ForInit ; Expression ; ForUpdateopt ) Statement
```

which in turn is an abbreviation for:

```
BasicForStatement:
     for (; ;) Statement
     for (; ; ForUpdate ) Statement
     for (; Expression ;) Statement
```

```
        for (; Expression ; ForUpdate ) Statement
        for ( ForInit ; ;) Statement
        for ( ForInit ; ; ForUpdate ) Statement
        for ( ForInit ; Expression ;) Statement
        for ( ForInit ; Expression ; ForUpdate
) Statement
```

so the nonterminal *BasicForStatement* actually has eight alternative right-hand sides. A very long right-hand side may be continued on a second line by substantially indenting this second line, as in:

```
   ConstructorDeclaration:
                      ConstructorModifiersopt
ConstructorDeclarator
                      Throwsopt ConstructorBody
```

which defines one right-hand side for the nonterminal *ConstructorDeclaration*.

When the words "one of" follow the colon in a grammar definition, they signify that each of the terminal symbols on the following line or lines is an alternative definition. For example, the lexical grammar contains the production:

```
ZeroToThree: one of
        0 1 2 3
```

which is merely a convenient abbreviation for:

```
ZeroToThree:
        0 1 2 3
```

When an alternative in a lexical production appears to be a token, it represents the sequence of characters that would make up such a token. Thus, the definition:

```
BooleanLiteral: one of
        true false
```

in a lexical grammar production is shorthand for:

```
BooleanLiteral:
        t r u e
        f a l s e
```

The right-hand side of a lexical production may specify that certain expansions are not permitted by using the phrase "but not" and then indicating the expansions to be excluded, as in the productions for *InputCharacter* and *Identifier*

```
InputCharacter:
        UnicodeInputCharacter but not CR or LF
Identifier:
        IdentifierName but not a Keyword or Boolean
Literal or NullLiteral
```

Finally, a few nonterminal symbols are described by a descriptive phrase in roman type in cases where it would be impractical to list all the alternatives:

```
RawInputCharacter:
        any Unicode character
```

LEXICAL STRUCTURE

Programs are written using the Unicode character set. Information about this character set and its associated character encodings. The Java platform tracks the Unicode specification as it evolves. The precise version of Unicode used by a given release is specified in the documentation of the class `Character`.

Versions of the Java programming language prior to 1.1 used Unicode version 1.1.5. Upgrades to newer versions of the Unicode Standard occurred in JDK 1.1 (to Unicode 2.0), JDK 1.1.7 (to Unicode 2.1), J2SE 1.4 (to Unicode 3.0), and J2SE 5.0. The Unicode standard was originally designed as a fixed-width 16-bit character encoding.

It has since been changed to allow for characters whose representation requires more than 16 bits. The range of legal code points is now U+0000 to U+10FFFF, using the hexadecimal U+n notation. Characters whose code points are greater than U+FFFF are called supplementary characters. To represent the complete range of characters using only 16-bit units, the Unicode standard defines an encoding called UTF-16.

In this encoding, supplementary characters are represented as pairs of 16-bit code units, the first from the high-surrogates range, (U+D800 to U+DBFF), the second from the low-surrogates range (U+DC00 to U+DFFF). For characters in the range U+0000 to U+FFFF, the values of code points and UTF-16 code units are the same. The Java programming language represents text in sequences of 16-bit code units, using the UTF-

16 encoding. A few APIs, primarily in the `Character` class, use 32-bit integers to represent code points as individual entities. The Java platform provides methods to convert between the two representations. This book uses the terms code point and UTF-16 code unit where the representation is relevant, and the generic term character where the representation is irrelevant to the discussion.

Except for comments, identifiers, and the contents of character and string literals, all input elements in a program are formed only from ASCII characters (or Unicode escapes which result in ASCII characters). ASCII (ANSI X3.4) is the American Standard Code for Information Interchange. The first 128 characters of the Unicode character encoding are the ASCII characters.

TRANSLATIONS

A raw Unicode character stream is translated into a sequence of tokens, using the following three lexical translation steps, which are applied in turn:

1. A translation of Unicode escapes in the raw stream of Unicode characters to the corresponding Unicode character. A Unicode escape of the form \u*xxxx*, where *xxxx* is a hexadecimal value, represents the UTF-16 code unit whose encoding is *xxxx*. This translation step allows any program to be expressed using only ASCII characters.
2. A translation of the Unicode stream resulting from step 1 into a stream of input characters and line terminators.
3. A translation of the stream of input characters and line terminators resulting from step 2 into a sequence of input elements which, after white space and comments are discarded, comprise the tokens that are the terminal symbols of the syntactic grammar.

The longest possible translation is used at each step, even if the result does not ultimately make a correct program while another lexical translation would. Thus the input characters **`a--b`** are tokenized as **`a`**, **`--`**, **`b`**, which is not part of any grammatically correct program, even though the tokenization **a, -, -, b** could be part of a grammatically correct program.

UNICODE ESCAPES

Implementations first recognize *Unicode escapes* in their input, translating the ASCII characters **\u** followed by four hexadecimal digits to the UTF-16 code unit with the indicated hexadecimal value, and passing all other characters unchanged. Representing supplementary characters requires two consecutive Unicode escapes. This translation step results in a sequence of Unicode input characters:

```
UnicodeInputCharacter:
    UnicodeEscape
    RawInputCharacter
UnicodeEscape:
    \ UnicodeMarker HexDigit HexDigit
HexDigit HexDigit
UnicodeMarker:
    u
    UnicodeMarker u
RawInputCharacter:
    any Unicode character
HexDigit: one of
0 1 2 3 4 5 6 7 8 9 a b c d e f A B C D E F
```

The ****, **u**, and hexadecimal digits here are all ASCII characters.

In addition to the processing implied by the grammar, for each raw input character that is a backslash \, input processing must consider how many other \ characters contiguously precede it, separating it from a non-\ character or the start of the input stream. If this number is even, then the \ is eligible to begin a Unicode escape; if the number is odd, then the \ is not eligible to begin a Unicode escape. For example, the raw input **"\\u2297=\u2297"** results in the eleven characters **" \ \ u 2 2 9 7 = ⊗ "** (**\u2297** is the Unicode encoding of the character "⊗"). If an eligible \ is not followed by **u**, then it is treated as a *RawInputCharacter* and remains part of the escaped

Unicode stream. If an eligible \ is followed by **u**, or more than one **u**, and the last **u** is not followed by four hexadecimal digits, then a compile-time error occurs. The character produced by a Unicode escape does not participate in further Unicode escapes. For example, the raw input **\u005cu005a** results in the six characters **\ u 0 0 5 a**, because **005c** is the Unicode value for \. It does not result in the character **Z**, which is Unicode character **005a**, because the \ that resulted from the **\u005c** is not interpreted as the start of a further Unicode escape.

The Java programming language specifies a standard way of transforming a program written in Unicode into ASCII that changes a program into a form that can be processed by ASCII-based tools. The transformation involves converting any Unicode escapes in the source text of the program to ASCII by adding an extra **u**-for example, **\u***xxxx* becomes **\uu***xxxx*-while simultaneously converting non-ASCII characters in the source text to Unicode escapes containing a single **u** each. This transformed version is equally acceptable to a compiler for the Java programming language ("Java compiler") and represents the exact same program.

The exact Unicode source can later be restored from this ASCII form by converting each escape sequence where multiple **u**'s are present to a sequence of Unicode characters with one fewer **u**, while simultaneously converting each escape sequence with a single **u** to the corresponding single Unicode character. Implementations should use the **\u***xxxx* notation as an output format to display Unicode characters when a suitable font is not available.

LINE TERMINATORS

Implementations next divide the sequence of Unicode input characters into lines by recognizing *line terminators*. This definition of lines determines the line numbers produced by a Java compiler or other system component. It also specifies the termination of the // form of a comment.

LineTerminator:

the ASCII LF **character, also known as "newline"**

the ASCII CR character, also known as "return"

the ASCII CR character followed by the ASCII LF character

InputCharacter:

UnicodeInputCharacter but not CR or LF

Lines are terminated by the ASCII characters **CR**, or **LF**, or **CR LF**. The two characters **CR** immediately followed by **LF** are counted as one line terminator, not two.

The result is a sequence of line terminators and input characters, which are the terminal symbols for the third step in the tokenization process.

INPUT ELEMENTS AND TOKENS

The input characters and line terminators that result from escape processing and then input line recognition are reduced to a sequence of *input elements*. Those input elements that are not white space or comments are *tokens*. The tokens are the terminal symbols of the syntactic grammar.

This process is specified by the following productions:

```
Input:
    InputElementsopt Subopt
InputElements:
    InputElement
    InputElements InputElement
InputElement:
    WhiteSpace
    Comment
    Token
Token:
    Identifier
    Keyword
    Literal
    Separator
    Operator
Sub:
    the ASCII SUB character, also known as "control-Z"
```

White space and comments can serve to separate tokens that, if adjacent, might be tokenized in another manner. For example, the ASCII characters `-` and `=` in the input can form the operator token `-=` only if there is no intervening white space or comment. As a special concession for compatibility with certain operating systems, the ASCII SUB character (`\u001a`, or control-Z) is ignored if it is the last character in the escaped input stream. Consider two tokens *x* and *y* in the resulting input stream. If *x* precedes *y*, then we say that *x* is *to the left of y* and that *y* is *to the right of x*.

For example, in this simple piece of code:

```
class Empty {
}
```

we say that the } token is to the right of the { token, even though it appears, in this two-dimensional representation on paper, downward and to the left of the { token. This convention about the use of the words left and right allows us to speak, for example, of the right-hand operand of a binary operator or of the left-hand side of an assignment.

WHITE SPACE

White space is defined as the ASCII space, horizontal tab, and form feed characters, as well as line terminators.

```
WhiteSpace:
the ASCII SP character, also known as "space"
the ASCII HT character, also known as "horizontal tab"
the ASCII FF character, also known as "form feed"
LineTerminator
```

COMMENTS

There are two kinds of *comments*:

`/* text */`	A traditional comment: all the text from the ASCII characters`/*` to the ASCII characters `*/` is ignored (as

	in C and C++).
// text	A end-of-line comment: all the text from the ASCII characters// to the end of the line is ignored (as in C++).

These comments are formally specified by the following productions:

```
Comment:
    TraditionalComment
    EndOfLineComment
TraditionalComment:
    / * CommentTail
EndOfLineComment:
    / / CharactersInLineopt
CommentTail:
    * CommentTailStar
    NotStar CommentTail
CommentTailStar:
    /
    * CommentTailStar
    NotStarNotSlash CommentTail
NotStar:
    InputCharacter but not *
    LineTerminator
NotStarNotSlash:
    InputCharacter but not * or /
    LineTerminator
CharactersInLine:
    InputCharacter
    CharactersInLine InputCharacter
```

These productions imply all of the following properties:

- Comments do not nest.
- /* and */ have no special meaning in comments that begin with //.
- // has no special meaning in comments that begin with /* or /**.

As a result, the text:

```
/* this comment /* // /** ends here: */
```

is a single complete comment.

The lexical grammar implies that comments do not occur within character literals or string literals.

IDENTIFIERS

An *identifier* is an unlimited-length sequence of *Java letters* and *Java digits*, the first of which must be a Java letter. An identifier cannot have the same spelling (Unicode character sequence) as a keyword, boolean literal, or the null literal.

```
Identifier:
        IdentifierChars but not a Keyword or BooleanLiteral or NullLiteral
IdentifierChars:
        JavaLetter
        IdentifierChars JavaLetterOrDigit
JavaLetter:
        any Unicode character that is a Java letter
JavaLetterOrDigit:
        any Unicode character that is a Java letter-or-digit.
```

Letters and digits may be drawn from the entire Unicode character set, which supports most writing scripts in use in the world today, including the large sets for Chinese, Japanese, and Korean. This allows programmers to use identifiers in their programs that are written in their native languages. A "Java letter" is a character for which the method `Character.isJavaIdentifierStart(int)` returns `true`. A "Java letter-or-digit" is a character for which the method `Character.isJavaIdentifierPart(int)` returns `true`.

The Java letters include uppercase and lowercase ASCII Latin letters `A-Z` (`\u0041-\u005a`), and `a-z` (`\u0061-\u007a`), and, for historical reasons, the ASCII underscore (_, or `\u005f`) and dollar sign (`$`, or `\u0024`). The `$` character should be used only in mechanically generated source code or, rarely, to access preexisting names on legacy systems.

The "Java digits" include the ASCII digits `0-9` (`\u0030-\u0039`). Two identifiers are the same only if they are identical, that is, have the same Unicode character for each letter or digit. Identifiers that have the same external appearance may yet be different. For example, the identifiers consisting of the single letters LATIN CAPITAL LETTER A (`A`, `\u0041`), LATIN SMALL LETTER A (`a`, `\u0061`), GREEK CAPITAL LETTER ALPHA (`A`, `\u0391`), CYRILLIC SMALL LETTER A (`a`, `\u0430`) and MATHEMATICAL BOLD ITALIC SMALL A (`a`, `\ud835\udc82`) are all different. Unicode composite characters are different from the decomposed characters.

For example, a LATIN CAPITAL LETTER A ACUTE (`Á`, `\u00c1`) could be considered to be the same as a LATIN CAPITAL LETTER A (`A`, `\u0041`) immediately followed by a NON-SPACING ACUTE (´, `\u0301`) when sorting, but these are different in identifiers. **`String i3 αρετη MAX_VALUE is Letter OrDigit.`**

KEYWORDS

The following character sequences, formed from ASCII letters, are reserved for use as *keywords* and cannot be used as identifiers:

```
Keyword: one of

abstract  continue  for         new        switch
assert    default   if          package    synchronized
boolean   do        goto        private    this
break     double    implements  protected  throw
byte      else      import      public     throws
case      enum      instanceof  return     transient
catch     extends   int         short      try
char      final     interface   static     void
class     finally   long        strictfp   volatile
const     float     native      super      while
```

The keywords `const` and `goto` are reserved, even though they are not currently used. This may allow a Java compiler to produce better error messages if these C++ keywords incorrectly appear in programs. While **`true`** and **`false`** might appear to be keywords, they are technically Boolean literals.Similarly, while **`null`** might appear to be a keyword, it is technically the null literal.

LITERALS

A *literal* is the source code representation of a value of a primitive type, the **`String`** type, or the null type:

```
Literal:
     IntegerLiteral
     FloatingPointLiteral
     BooleanLiteral
     CharacterLiteral
     StringLiteral
     NullLiteral
```

INTEGER LITERALS

For a general discussion of the integer types and values.

An *integer literal* may be expressed in decimal (base 10), hexadecimal (base 16), or octal (base 8):

```
IntegerLiteral:
     DecimalIntegerLiteral
     HexIntegerLiteral
     OctalIntegerLiteral
DecimalIntegerLiteral:
     DecimalNumeral  IntegerTypeSuffixopt
HexIntegerLiteral:
     HexNumeral  IntegerTypeSuffixopt
OctalIntegerLiteral:
     OctalNumeral  IntegerTypeSuffixopt
IntegerTypeSuffix: one of
l L
```

An integer literal is of type **`long`** if it is suffixed with an ASCII letter `L` or `l` (ell); otherwise it is of type **`int`**. The suffix `L` is preferred, because the letter `l` (ell) is often hard to distinguish from the digit `1` (one).

A decimal numeral is either the single ASCII character `0`, representing the integer zero, or consists of an ASCII digit from

`1` to `9`, optionally followed by one or more ASCII digits from `0` to `9`, representing a positive integer:

```
DecimalNumeral:
    0
    NonZeroDigit Digitsopt
Digits:
    Digit
    Digits Digit
Digit:
    0
    NonZeroDigit
NonZeroDigit: one of
    1 2 3 4 5 6 7 8 9
```

A hexadecimal numeral consists of the leading ASCII characters `0x` or `0X` followed by one or more ASCII hexadecimal digits and can represent a positive, zero, or negative integer. Hexadecimal digits with values 10 through 15 are represented by the ASCII letters `a` through `f` or `A` through `F`, respectively; each letter used as a hexadecimal digit may be uppercase or lowercase.

```
HexNumeral:
    0 x HexDigits
    0 X HexDigits
HexDigits:
    HexDigit
    HexDigit HexDigits
```

The following production from is repeated here for clarity:

```
HexDigit: one of
0 1 2 3 4 5 6 7 8 9 a b c d e f A B C D E F
```

An octal numeral consists of an ASCII digit `0` followed by one or more of the ASCII digits `0` through `7` and can represent a positive, zero, or negative integer.

```
OctalNumeral:
    0 OctalDigits
OctalDigits:
    OctalDigit
    OctalDigit OctalDigits
OctalDigit: one of
```

`0 1 2 3 4 5 6 7`

Note that octal numerals always consist of two or more digits; `0` is always considered to be a decimal numeral-not that it matters much in practice, for the numerals `0`, `00`, and `0x0` all represent exactly the same integer value.

The largest decimal literal of type `int` is `2147483648` (2^{31}). All decimal literals from `0` to `2147483647` may appear anywhere an `int` literal may appear, but the literal `2147483648` may appear only as the operand of the unary negation operator `-`. The largest positive hexadecimal and octal literals of type `int` are `0x7fffffff` and `017777777777`, respectively, which equal `2147483647` (2^{31}-1). The most negative hexadecimal and octal literals of type `int` are `0x80000000` and `020000000000`, respectively, each of which represents the decimal value `-2147483648` (-2^{31}). The hexadecimal and octal literals `0xffffffff` and `037777777777`, respectively, represent the decimal value `-1`.

A compile-time error occurs if a decimal literal of type `int` is larger than `2147483648` (2^{31}), or if the literal `2147483648` appears anywhere other than as the operand of the unary - operator, or if a hexadecimal or octal `int` literal does not fit in 32 bits.

Examples of `int` literals:

`0 2 0372 0xDadaCafe 1996 0x0 0FF00FF` The largest decimal literal of type `long` is `9223372036854775808L` (2^{63}). All decimal literals from `0L` to `9223372036854775807L` may appear anywhere a `long` literal may appear, but the literal `9223372036854775808L` may appear only as the operand of the unary negation operator. The largest positive hexadecimal and octal literals of type `long` are `0x7fffffffffffffffL` and `0777777777777777777777L`, respectively, which equal `9223372036854775807L` (2^{63}-1).

The literals `0x8000000000000000L` and `01000000000000000000000L` are the most negative `long` hexadecimal and octal literals, respectively. Each has the decimal value `-9223372036854775808L` (-2^{63}). The hexadecimal and octal literals `0xffffffffffffffffL` and `01777777777777777777777L`, respectively, represent the decimal value `-1L`. A compile-time error occurs if a decimal literal of type `long` is larger than `9223372036854775808L` (2^{63}), or if the literal `9223372036854775808L` appears anywhere other than as the operand of the unary - operator, or if a hexadecimal or octal `long` literal does not fit in 64 bits. Examples of `long` literals:

```
01 0777L 0x100000000L 2147483648L 0xC0B0L
```

FLOATING-POINT LITERALS

A *floating-point literal* has the following parts: a whole-number part, a decimal or hexadecimal point (represented by an ASCII period character), a fractional part, an exponent, and a type suffix. A floating point number may be written either as a decimal value or as a hexadecimal value. For decimal literals, the exponent, if present, is indicated by the ASCII letter `e` or `E` followed by an optionally signed integer. For hexadecimal literals, the exponent is always required and is indicated by the ASCII letter `p` or `P` followed by an optionally signed integer.

For decimal floating-point literals, at least one digit, in either the whole number or the fraction part, and either a decimal point, an exponent, or a float type suffix are required. All other parts are optional. For hexadecimal floating-point literals, at least one digit is required in either the whole number or fraction part, the exponent is mandatory, and the float type suffix is optional.

A floating-point literal is of type `float` if it is suffixed with an ASCII letter `F` or `f`; otherwise its type is `double` and it can optionally be suffixed with an ASCII letter `D` or `d`.

```
   FloatingPointLiteral:
       DecimalFloatingPointLiteral
       HexadecimalFloatingPointLiteral
   DecimalFloatingPointLiteral:
       Digits. Digitsopt ExponentPartopt
FloatTypeSuffixopt
       . Digits ExponentPartopt
FloatTypeSuffixopt
       Digits ExponentPart FloatTypeSuffixopt
       Digits ExponentPartopt FloatTypeSuffix
```

```
ExponentPart:
    ExponentIndicator SignedInteger
ExponentIndicator: one of
    e E
SignedInteger:
    Signopt Digits
Sign: one of
    + -
FloatTypeSuffix: one of
    f F d D
HexadecimalFloatingPointLiteral:
    HexSignificand BinaryExponent
FloatTypeSuffixopt
HexSignificand:
    HexNumeral
    HexNumeral.
    0x HexDigitsopt. HexDigits
    0X HexDigitsopt. HexDigits
BinaryExponent:
    BinaryExponentIndicator SignedInteger
BinaryExponentIndicator:one of
    p P
```

The elements of the types **`float`** and **`double`** are those values that can be represented using the IEEE 754 32-bit single-precision and 64-bit double-precision binary floating-point formats, respectively.

The details of proper input conversion from a Unicode string representation of a floating-point number to the internal IEEE 754 binary floating-point representation are described for the methods `valueOf` of class `Float` and class `Double` of the package `java.lang`.

The largest positive finite `float` literal is `3.4028235e38f`. The smallest positive finite nonzero literal of type `float` is `1.40e-45f`. The largest positive finite `double` literal is `1.7976931348623157e308`. The smallest positive finite nonzero literal of type `double` is `4.9e-324`.

A compile-time error occurs if a nonzero floating-point literal is too large, so that on rounded conversion to its internal representation it becomes an IEEE 754 infinity. A program can represent infinities without producing a compile-time error by using constant expressions such as `1f/0f` or `-1d/0d` or by using the predefined constants `POSITIVE_INFINITY` and `NEGATIVE_INFINITY` of the classes `Float` and `Double`.

A compile-time error occurs if a nonzero floating-point literal is too small, so that, on rounded conversion to its internal representation, it becomes a zero. A compile-time error does not occur if a nonzero floating-point literal has a small value that, on rounded conversion to its internal representation, becomes a nonzero denormalized number.

Predefined constants representing Not-a-Number values are defined in the classes `Float` and `Double` as `Float.NaN` and `Double.NaN`.

Examples of `float` literals:

```
1e1f 2.f.3f 0f 3.14f 6.022137e+23f
```

Examples of `double` literals:

```
1e1 2..3 0.0 3.14 1e-9d 1e137
```

Besides expressing floating-point values in decimal and hexadecimal, the method `intBitsToFloat` of class `Float` and method `longBitsToDouble` of class `Double` provide a way to express floating-point values in terms of hexadecimal or octal integer literals.For example, the value of:

```
Double.longBitsToDouble(0x400921FB54442D18L)
```

is equal to the value of `Math.PI`.

BOOLEAN LITERALS

The `boolean` type has two values, represented by the literals `true` and `false`, formed from ASCII letters.

A *boolean literal* is always of type `boolean`.

```
BooleanLiteral: one of true false
```

CHARACTER LITERALS

A *character literal* is expressed as a character or an escape sequence, enclosed in ASCII single quotes. (The single-quote, or apostrophe, character is `\u0027`.) Character literals can only represent UTF-16 code units, *i.e.*, they are limited to values from `\u0000` to `\uffff`. Supplementary characters must be represented either as a surrogate pair within a char sequence, or as an integer, depending on the API they are used with.

A character literal is always of type **char**.

```
CharacterLiteral:
        ' SingleCharacter '
        ' EscapeSequence '
SingleCharacter:
        InputCharacter but not ' or \
```

The escape sequences are described in.

As specified in, the characters CR and LF are never an *InputCharacter*; they are recognized as constituting a *LineTerminator*.

It is a compile-time error for the character following the *SingleCharacter* or *EscapeSequence* to be other than a **'**.

It is a compile-time error for a line terminator to appear after the opening **'** and before the closing **'**.

The following are examples of **char** literals:

```
'a'
'%'
'\t'
'\\'
'\''
'\u03a9'
'\uFFFF'
'\177'
'W'
'Ä'
```

Because Unicode escapes are processed very early, it is not correct to write **'\u000a'** for a character literal whose value is linefeed (LF); the Unicode escape **\u000a** is transformed into an actual linefeed in translation step 1 and the linefeed becomes a *LineTerminator* in step 2, and so the character literal is not valid in step 3.

Instead, one should use the escape sequence **'\n'**.Similarly, it is not correct to write **'\u000d'** for a character literal whose value is carriage return (CR). Instead, use **'\r'**. In C and C++, a character literal may contain representations of more than one character, but the value of such a character literal is implementation-defined. In the Java programming language, a character literal always represents exactly one character.

STRING LITERALS

A *string literal* consists of zero or more characters enclosed in double quotes. Characters may be represented by escape sequences - one escape sequence for characters in the range U+0000 to U+FFFF, two escape sequences for the UTF-16 surrogate code units of characters in the range U+010000 to U+10FFFF.

A string literal is always of type `String`. A string literal always refers to the same instance of class `String`.

```
StringLiteral:
        " StringCharactersopt "
StringCharacters:
        StringCharacter
        StringCharacters StringCharacter
StringCharacter:
        InputCharacter but not " or \
        EscapeSequence
```

The escape sequences are described in.

As specified in, neither of the characters CR and LF is ever considered to be an *InputCharacter*; each is recognized as constituting a *LineTerminator*. It is a compile-time error for a line terminator to appear after the opening `"` and before the closing matching `"`. A long string literal can always be broken up into shorter pieces and written as a (possibly parenthesized) expression using the string concatenation operator `+`.

The following are examples of string literals:

```
""// the empty string
"\""// a string containing " alone
"This is a string"// a string containing 16
characters
"This is a " +// actually a string-valued
constant expression,
"two-line string"// formed from two string
literals
```

Because Unicode escapes are processed very early, it is not correct to write **"\u000a"** for a string literal containing a single linefeed (LF); the Unicode escape **\u000a** is transformed into an actual linefeed in translation step 1 and the linefeed becomes a *LineTerminator* in step 2, and so the string literal is not valid in step 3. Instead, one should write **"\n"**. Similarly, it is not correct to write **"\u000d"** for a string literal containing a single carriage return (CR). Instead use **"\r"**.

Each string literal is a reference to an instance of class **String**. **String** objects have a constant value. String literals-or, more generally, strings that are the values of constant expressions -are "interned" so as to share unique instances, using the method **String.intern**.

Thus, the test program consisting of the compilation unit:

```
package testPackage;
class Test {
public static void main(String[] args) {
String hello = "Hello", lo = "lo";
System.out.print((hello == "Hello") + " ");
System.out.print((Other.hello == hello) + "
");
System.out.print((other.Other.hello == hello)
+ " ");
System.out.print((hello == ("Hel"+"lo")) + "
");
System.out.print((hello == ("Hel"+lo)) + "
");
System.out.println(hello == ("Hel"+lo).
intern());
}
}
class Other {static String hello = "Hello";}
```

and the compilation unit:

```
package other;
public class Other {static String hello =
"Hello";}
```

produces the output:

```
true true true true false true
```

This example illustrates six points:

- Literal strings within the same class in the same package represent references to the same **String** object.
- Literal strings within different classes in the same package represent references to the same **String** object.
- Literal strings within different classes in different packages likewise represent references to the same **String** object.
- Strings computed by constant expressions are computed at compile time and then treated as if they were literals.
- Strings computed by concatenation at run time are newly created and therefore distinct.

The result of explicitly interning a computed string is the same string as any pre-existing literal string with the same contents.

ESCAPE SEQUENCES FOR CHARACTER AND STRING LITERALS

The character and string *escape sequences* allow for the representation of some nongraphic characters as well as the single quote, double quote, and backslash characters in character literals and string literals.

```
    EscapeSequence:
    \ b/* \u0008: backspace BS */
    \ t/* \u0009: horizontal tab HT */
    \ n/* \u000a: linefeed LF */
    \ f/* \u000c: form feed FF */
    \ r/* \u000d: carriage return CR */
    \ "/* \u0022: double quote " */
    \ '/* \u0027: single quote ' */
    \ \/* \u005c: backslash \ */
    OctalEscape/* \u0000 to \u00ff: from octal
value */
    OctalEscape:
    \ OctalDigit
```

```
\ OctalDigit OctalDigit
\ ZeroToThree OctalDigit OctalDigit
OctalDigit: one of
0 1 2 3 4 5 6 7
ZeroToThree: one of
0 1 2 3
```

It is a compile-time error if the character following a backslash in an escape is not an ASCII `b`, `t`, `n`, `f`, `r`, `"`, `'`, `\`, `0`, `1`, `2`, `3`, `4`, `5`, `6`, or `7`. The Unicode escape `\u` is processed earlier. (Octal escapes are provided for compatibility with C, but can express only Unicode values `\u0000` through `\u00FF`, so Unicode escapes are usually preferred.)

THE NULL LITERAL

The null type has one value, the null reference, represented by the literal `null`, which is formed from ASCII characters. A *null literal* is always of the null type.

```
NullLiteral:
null
```

SEPARATORS

The following nine ASCII characters are the *separators* (punctuators):

```
Separator: one of
    ( ) { } [ ] ; .
```

OPERATORS

The following 37 tokens are the *operators,* formed from ASCII characters:

```
Operator: one of
=   >   <   !   ~   ?   :
==  <=  >=  !=  &&  ||  ++  --
+   -   *   /   &   |   ^   %   <<   >>   >>>
+=  -=  *=  /=  &=  |=  ^=  %=  <<=  >>=  >>>=
```

2

Variables

INTRODUCTION

The Java programming language is a *strongly typed* language, which means that every variable and every expression has a type that is known at compile time. Types limit the values that a variable can hold or that an expression can produce, limit the operations supported on those values, and determine the meaning of the operations. Strong typing helps detect errors at compile time.

The types of the Java programming language are divided into two categories: primitive types and reference types. The primitive types are the **`boolean`** type and the numeric types. The numeric types are the integral types **`byte`**, **`short`**, **`int`**, **`long`**, and **`char`**, and the floating-point types **`float`** and **`double`**. The reference types are class types, interface types, and array types.

There is also a special null type. An object is a dynamically created instance of a class type or a dynamically created array. The values of a reference type are references to objects. All objects, including arrays, support the methods of class **`Object`**. String literals are represented by **`String`** objects.

Types exist at compile-time. Some types correspond to classes and interfaces, which exist at run-time. The correspondence between types and classes or interfaces is incomplete for two reasons:

1. At run-time, classes and interfaces are loaded by the Java virtual machine using class loaders. Each class loader defines its own set of classes and interfaces. As a result, it is possible for two loaders to load an

identical class or interface definition but produce distinct classes or interfaces at run-time.

2. Type arguments and type variables are not reified at run-time. As a result, different parametreized types are implemented by the same class or interface at run time. Indeed, all invocations of a given generic type declaration share a single run-time implementation.

A consequence of is the possibility of heap pollution. Under certain conditions, it is possible that a variable of a parametreized type refers to an object that is not of that parametreized type. The variable will always refer to an object that is an instance of a class that implements the parametreized type.

THE KINDS OF TYPES AND VALUES

There are two kinds of *types* in the Java programming language: primitive types and reference types. There are, correspondingly, two kinds of data values that can be stored in variables, passed as arguments, returned by methods, and operated on: primitive values and reference values.

```
Type:
    PrimitiveType
    ReferenceType
```

There is also a special *null type,* the type of the expression null, which has no name. Because the null type has no name, it is impossible to declare a variable of the null type or to cast to the null type.

The null reference is the only possible value of an expression of null type. The null reference can always be cast to any reference type. In practice, the programmer can ignore the null type and just pretend that null is merely a special literal that can be of any reference type.

PRIMITIVE TYPES AND VALUES

A *primitive type* is predefined by the Java programming language and named by its reserved keyword:

```
PrimitiveType:
```

```
NumericType
boolean
NumericType:
IntegralType
FloatingPointType
IntegralType: one of
byte short int long char
FloatingPointType: one of
float double
```

Primitive values do not share state with other primitive values. A variable whose type is a primitive type always holds a primitive value of that same type. The value of a variable of primitive type can be changed only by assignment operations on that variable including increment and decrement operators. The *numeric types* are the integral types and the floating-point types. The *integral types* are **`byte`**, **`short`**, **`int`**, and **`long`**, whose values are 8-bit, 16-bit, 32-bit and 64-bit signed two's-complement integers, respectively, and **`char`**, whose values are 16-bit unsigned integers representing UTF-16 code units. The *floating-point types* are **`float`**, whose values include the 32-bit IEEE 754 floating-point numbers, and **`double`**, whose values include the 64-bit IEEE 754 floating-point numbers. The **`boolean`** type has exactly two values: **`true`** and **`false`**.

INTEGRAL TYPES AND VALUES

The values of the integral types are integers in the following ranges:

- For byte, from -128 to 127, inclusive
- For short, from -32768 to 32767, inclusive
- For int, from -2147483648 to 2147483647, inclusive
- For long, from -9223372036854775808 to 9223372036854775807, inclusive
- For char, from '\u0000' to '\uffff' inclusive, that is, from 0 to 65535

INTEGER OPERATIONS

The Java programming language provides a number of operators that act on integral values:

- The comparison operators, which result in a value of type boolean:
  - The numerical comparison operators <, <=, >, and >=
  - The numerical equality operators == and !=
- The numerical operators, which result in a value of type int or long:
  - The unary plus and minus operators + and -
  - The multiplicative operators *, /, and %
  - The additive operators + and -
  - The increment operator ++, both prefix and postfix
  - The decrement operator —, both prefix and postfix
  - The signed and unsigned shift operators <<, >>, and >>>
  - The bitwise complement operator ~
  - The integer bitwise operators &, |, and ^
- The conditional operator ?:
- The cast operator, which can convert from an integral value to a value of any specified numeric type
- The string concatenation operator + which, when given a String operand and an integral operand, will convert the integral operand to a String representing its value in decimal form, and then produce a newly created String that is the concatenation of the two strings

Other useful constructors, methods, and constants are predefined in the classes **`Byte`**, **`Short`**, **`Integer`**, **`Long`**, and **`Character`**.

If an integer operator other than a shift operator has at least one operand of type **`long`**, then the operation is carried out using 64-bit precision, and the result of the numerical operator is of type **`long`**. If the other operand is not **`long`**, it is first widened to type **`long`** by numeric promotion.

Otherwise, the operation is carried out using 32-bit precision, and the result of the numerical operator is of type **`int`**. If either operand is not an **`int`**, it is first widened to type **`int`** by numeric promotion. The built-in integer operators do not indicate overflow or underflow in any way. Integer operators can throw a **NullPointerException** if unboxing conversion of a null reference is required. Other than that, the only integer operators that can throw an exception are the integer divide operator / and the integer remainder operator %, which throw an **ArithmeticException** if the right-hand operand is zero, and the increment and decrement operators ++ and – which can throw an **OutOfMemoryError** if boxing conversion is required and there is not sufficient memory available to perform the conversion.

The example:

```
class Test {
public static void main(String[] args) {
        int i = 1000000;
        System.out.println(i * i);
        long l = i;
        System.out.println(l * l);
        System.out.println(20296/ (l - i));
        }
}
```

```
produces the output:
-727379968
1000000000000
```

and then encounters an **ArithmeticException** in the division by l - i, because l - i is zero. The first multiplication is performed in 32-bit precision, whereas the second multiplication is a long multiplication. The value -727379968 is the decimal value of the low 32 bits of the mathematical result, 1000000000000, which is a value too large for type **int**.

Any value of any integral type may be cast to or from any numeric type. There are no casts between integral types and the type boolean.

FLOATING-POINT TYPES, FORMATS, AND VALUES

The floating-point types are **float** and **double**, which are conceptually associated with the single-precision 32-bit and double-precision 64-bit format IEEE 754 values and operations as specified in *IEEE Standard for Binary Floating-Point Arithmetic,* ANSI/IEEE Standard 754-1985 (IEEE, New York). The IEEE 754 standard includes not only positive and negative numbers that consist of a sign and magnitude, but also positive and negative zeros, positive and negative *infinities,* and special *Not-a-Number* values (hereafter abbreviated NaN). A NaN value is used to represent the result of certain invalid operations such as dividing zero by zero.

NaN constants of both `float` and `double` type are predefined as `Float.NaN` and `Double.NaN`. Every implementation of the Java programming language is required to support two standard sets of floating-point values, called the *float value set* and the *double value set*. In addition, an implementation of the Java programming language may support either or both of two extended-exponent floating-point value sets, called the *float-extended-exponent value set* and the *double-extended-exponent value set.*

These extended-exponent value sets may, under certain circumstances, be used instead of the standard value sets to represent the values of expressions of type `float` or `double`. The finite nonzero values of any floating-point value set can all be expressed in the form $s \cdot m \cdot 2^{(e-N+1)}$, where s is +1 or -1, m is a positive integer less than 2^N, and e is an integer between $E_{min} = -(2^{K-1}-2)$ and $E_{max} = 2^{K-1}-1$, inclusive, and where N and K are parametres that depend on the value set. Some values can be represented in this form in more than one way; for example, supposing that a value v in a value set might be represented in this form using certain values for s, m, and e, then if it happened that m were even and e were less than 2^{K-1}, one could halve m and increase e by 1 to produce a second representation for the same value v. A representation in this form is called *normalized* if $m \geq 2^{(N-1)}$; otherwise the representation is said to be *denormalized.* If a value in a value set cannot be represented in such a way that $m \geq 2^{(N-1)}$, then the value is said to be a *denormalized value,* because it has no normalized representation. The constraints on the parametres N and K (and on the derived parametres E_{min} and E_{max}) for the two required and two optional floating-point value sets are summarized in Table.

Parametre	float	float-extended -exponent	double	double-extended -exponent
N	24	24	53	53
K	8	≥ 11	11	≥ 15
E_{max}	+127	$\geq +1023$	+1023	$\geq +16383$
E_{min}	-126	≤ -1022	–1022	≤ -16382

Where one or both extended-exponent value sets are supported by an implementation, then for each supported extended-exponent value set there is a specific implementation-dependent constant *K*, whose value is constrained by above Table; this value *K* in turn dictates the values for E_{min} and E_{max}.

Each of the four value sets includes not only the finite nonzero values that are ascribed to it above, but also NaN values and the four values positive zero, negative zero, positive infinity, and negative infinity.

Note that the constraints in above Table are designed so that every element of the float value set is necessarily also an element of the float-extended-exponent value set, the double value set, and the double-extended-exponent value set. Likewise, each element of the double value set is necessarily also an element of the double-extended-exponent value set. Each extended-exponent value set has a larger range of exponent values than the corresponding standard value set, but does not have more precision.

The elements of the float value set are exactly the values that can be represented using the single floating-point format defined in the IEEE 754 standard. The elements of the double value set are exactly the values that can be represented using the double floating-point format defined in the IEEE 754 standard. Note, however, that the elements of the float-extended-exponent and double-extended-exponent value sets defined here do *not* correspond to the values that can be represented using IEEE 754 single extended and double extended formats, respectively. The float, float-extended-exponent, double, and double-extended-exponent value sets are not types. It is always correct for an implementation of the Java programming language to use an element of the float value set to represent a value of type **`float`**; however, it may be permissible in certain regions of code for an implementation to use an element of the float-extended-exponent value set instead. Similarly, it is always correct for an implementation to use an element of the double value set to represent a value of type **`double`**; however, it may be permissible in certain regions of code for an implementation to use an element of the double-extended-exponent value set instead.

Except for NaN, floating-point values are *ordered*; arranged from smallest to largest, they are negative infinity, negative finite nonzero values, positive and negative zero, positive finite nonzero values, and positive infinity. IEEE 754 allows multiple distinct NaN values for each of its single and double floating-point formats.

While each hardware architecture returns a particular bit pattern for NaN when a new NaN is generated, a programmer can also create NaNs with different bit patterns to encode, for example, retrospective diagnostic information. For the most part, the Java platform treats NaN values of a given type as though collapsed into a single canonical value (and hence this specification normally refers to an arbitrary NaN as though to a canonical value).

However, version 1.3 the Java platform introduced methods enabling the programmer to distinguish between NaN values: the **`Float. float To Raw Int Bits`** and **`Double .double ToRaw LongBits`** methods. The interested reader is referred to the specifications for the **`Float`** and **`Double`** classes for more information.

Positive zero and negative zero compare equal; thus the result of the expression **`0.0==-0.0`** is **`true`** and the result of **`0.0>-0.0`** is **`false`**. But other operations can distinguish positive and negative zero; for example, **`1.0/0.0`** has the value positive infinity, while the value of **`1.0/-0.0`** is negative infinity.

NaN is *unordered,* so the numerical comparison operators **`<`**, **`<=`**, **`>`**, and **`>=`** return **`false`** if either or both operands are NaN. The equality operator **`==`** returns **`false`** if either operand is NaN, and the inequality operator **`!=`** returns **`true`** if either operand is NaN. In particular, `x!=x` is `true` if and only if `x` is NaN, and `(x<y) == !(x>=y)` will be `false` if `x` or `y` is NaN.

Any value of a floating-point type may be cast to or from any numeric type. There are no casts between floating-point types and the type `boolean`.

FLOATING-POINT OPERATIONS

The Java programming language provides a number of operators that act on floating-point values:

- The comparison operators, which result in a value of type boolean:
  - The numerical comparison operators <, <=, >, and >=
  - The numerical equality operators == and !=
- The numerical operators, which result in a value of type float or double:
  - The unary plus and minus operators + and -
  - The multiplicative operators *, /, and %
  - The additive operators + and -
  - The increment operator ++, both prefix and postfix
  - The decrement operator —, both prefix and postfix
- The conditional operator ?:
- The cast operator, which can convert from a floating-point value to a value of any specified numeric type)
- The string concatenation operator + which, when given a String operand and a floating-point operand, will convert the floating-point operand to a String representing its value in decimal form (without information loss), and then produce a newly created String by concatenating the two strings

Other useful constructors, methods, and constants are predefined in the classes `Float`, `Double`, and `Math`. If at least one of the operands to a binary operator is of floating-point type, then the operation is a floating-point operation, even if the other is integral. If at least one of the operands to a numerical operator is of type `double`, then the operation is carried out using 64-bit floating-point arithmetic, and the result of the numerical operator is a value of type **`double`**. (If the other operand is not a **`double`**, it is first widened to type **`double`** by numeric promotion Otherwise, the operation is carried out using 32-bit floating-point arithmetic, and the result of the numerical operator is a value of type **`float`**. If the other operand is not a **`float`**, it is first widened to type **`float`** by numeric promotion.

Operators on floating-point numbers behave as specified by IEEE 754 (with the exception of the remainder operator. In particular, the Java programming language requires support of IEEE 754 *denormalized* floating-point numbers and *gradual underflow,* which make it easier to prove desirable properties of particular numerical algorithms. Floating-point operations do not "flush to zero" if the calculated result is a denormalized number.

The Java programming language requires that floating-point arithmetic behave as if every floating-point operator rounded its floating-point result to the result precision. *Inexact* results must be rounded to the representable value nearest to the infinitely precise result; if the two nearest representable values are equally near, the one with its least significant bit zero is chosen. This is the IEEE 754 standard's default rounding mode known as *round to nearest.*

The language uses *round towards zero* when converting a floating value to an integer, which acts, in this case, as though the number were truncated, discarding the mantissa bits. Rounding towards zero chooses at its result the format's value closest to and no greater in magnitude than the infinitely precise result.

Floating-point operators can throw a **`NullPointerException`** if unboxing conversion of a null reference is required. Other than that, the only floating-point operators that can throw an exception are the increment and decrement operators **`++`** and **`–`**, which can throw an **`OutOfMemoryError`** if boxing conversion is required and there is not sufficient memory available to perform the conversion.

An operation that overflows produces a signed infinity, an operation that underflows produces a denormalized value or a signed zero, and an operation that has no mathematically definite result produces NaN. All numeric operations with NaN as an operand produce NaN as a result. As has already been described, NaN is unordered, so a numeric comparison operation involving one or two NaNs returns **false** and any **!=** comparison involving NaN returns **true**, including **x!=x** when **x** is NaN.

The example program:

```
class Test {
public static void main(String[] args) {
    // An example of overflow:
    double d = 1e308;
    System.out.print("overflow produces
infinity: ");
    System.out.println(d + "*10==" + d*10);
    // An example of gradual underflow:
    d = 1e-305 * Math.PI;
    System.out.print("gradual underflow: " +
    d + "\n ");
    for (int i = 0; i < 4; i++)
    System.out.print(" " + (d/= 100000));
    System.out.println();
    // An example of NaN:
    System.out.print("0.0/0.0 is Not-a-Number:
    ");
    d = 0.0/0.0;
    System.out.println(d);
    // An example of inexact results and
  rounding:
    System.out.print("inexact results with
  float:");
    for (int i = 0; i < 100; i++) {
      float z = 1.0f/ i;
      if (z * i != 1.0f)
    System.out.print(" " + i);
    }
```

```
      System.out.println();
      // Another example of inexact results and
      rounding:
      System.out.print("inexact results with
   double:");
      for (int i = 0; i < 100; i++) {
         double z = 1.0/ i;
         if (z * i != 1.0)
              System.out.print(" " + i);
      }
      System.out.println();
      // An example of cast to integer rounding:
      System.out.print("cast to int rounds
   toward 0: ");
      d = 12345.6;
      System.out.println((int)d + " " + (int)(-
      d));
      }
   }
   produces the output:
   overflow produces infinity: 1.0e+308*10=
=Infinity
   gradual underflow: 3.141592653589793E-305
   3.1415926535898E-310 3.141592653E-315 3.142E-
   320 0.0
   0.0/0.0 is Not-a-Number: NaN
   inexact results with float: 0 41 47 55 61 82
   83 94 97
   inexact results with double: 0 49 98
   cast to int rounds toward 0: 12345 -12345
```

This example demonstrates, among other things, that gradual underflow can result in a gradual loss of precision. The results when `i` is `0` involve division by zero, so that `z` becomes positive infinity, and `z * 0` is NaN, which is not equal to `1.0`.

THE BOOLEAN TYPE AND BOOLEAN VALUES

The `boolean` type represents a logical quantity with two

possible values, indicated by the literals **`true`** and **`false`**. The boolean operators are:

- The relational operators `==` and `!=`
- The logical-complement operator `!`
- The logical operators `&`, `^`, and `|`
- The conditional-and and conditional-or operators `&&` and `||`
- The conditional operator `?`
- The string concatenation operator `+`, which, when given a `String` operand and a boolean operand, will convert the boolean operand to a `String` (either `"true"` or `"false"`), and then produce a newly created `String` that is the concatenation of the two strings

Boolean expressions determine the control flow in several kinds of statements:

- The `if` statement
- The `while` statement
- The `do` statement
- The `for` statement

A `boolean` expression also determines which subexpression is evaluated in the conditional `?:` operator. Only `boolean` or `Boolean` expressions can be used in control flow statements and as the first operand of the conditional operator `?:`. An integer `x` can be converted to a `boolean`, following the C language convention that any nonzero value is `true`, by the expression `x!=0`.

An object reference `obj` can be converted to a `boolean`, following the C language convention that any reference other than `null` is `true`, by the expression `obj!=null`.

A cast of a `boolean` value to type `boolean` or `Boolean` is allowed; no other casts on type `boolean` are allowed. A `boolean` can be converted to a string by string conversion.

REFERENCE TYPES AND VALUES

There are three kinds of *reference types*: class types, interface types, and array types. Reference types may be parametreized with type arguments.

`ReferenceType:`

```
        ClassOrInterfaceType
        TypeVariable
        ArrayType
    ClassOrInterfaceType:
        ClassType
        InterfaceType
    ClassType:
        TypeDeclSpecifier TypeArgumentsopt
    InterfaceType:
        TypeDeclSpecifier TypeArgumentsopt
    TypeDeclSpecifier:
        TypeName
        ClassOrInterfaceType. Identifier
    TypeName:
        Identifier
        TypeName. Identifier
    TypeVariable:
        Identifier
    ArrayType:
        Type []
```

A class or interface type consists of a type declaration specifier, optionally followed by type arguments (in which case it is a parametreized type). Type arguments are described in. A type declaration specifier may be either a type name, or a class or interface type followed by "." and an identifier. In the latter case, the specifier has the form *T.id*, where *id* must be the simple name of an accessible member type of *T*, or a compile-time error occurs. The specifier denotes that member type.

The sample code:

```
    class Point {int[] metrics;}
    interface Move {void move(int deltax, int
deltay);}
```

declares a class type `Point`, an interface type `Move`, and uses an array type `int[]` (an array of `int`) to declare the field `metrics` of the class `Point`.

OBJECTS

An *object* is a *class instance* or an array.

The reference values (often just *references*) are *pointers* to these objects, and a special null reference, which refers to no object. A class instance is explicitly created by a class instance creation expression. An array is explicitly created by an array creation expression.

A new class instance is implicitly created when the string concatenation operator + is used in a non-constant expression, resulting in a new object of type `String`. A new array object is implicitly created when an array initializer expression is evaluated; this can occur when a class or interface is initialized, when a new instance of a class is created, or when a local variable declaration statement is executed.

New objects of the types Boolean, Byte, Short, Character, Integer, Long, Float and Double may be implicitly created by boxing conversion.

Many of these cases are illustrated in the following example:

```
class Point {
    int x, y;
    Point() {System.out.println("default");}
    Point(int x, int y) {this.x = x; this.y
    = y;}
    // A Point instance is explicitly created
    at class initialization time:
    static Point origin = new Point(0,0);
    // A String can be implicitly created by
    a + operator:
    public String toString() {
       return "(" + x + "," + y + ")";
    }
}
class Test {
    public static void main(String[] args) {
       // A Point is explicitly created
    using newInstance:
       Point p = null;
       try {
       p =
 (Point)Class.forName("Point").newInstance();
```

```
    } catch (Exception e) {
    System.out.println(e);
    }
    // An array is implicitly created by an
    array constructor:
    Point a[] = {new Point(0,0), new
Point(1,1)};
    // Strings are implicitly created by +
operators:
    System.out.println("p: " + p);
    System.out.println("a: {" + a[0] + ", "
                + a[1] + "}");
    // An array is explicitly created by an
    array creation expression:
    String sa[] = new String[2];
    sa[0] = "he"; sa[1] = "llo";
    System.out.println(sa[0] + sa[1]);
    }
}
which produces the output:
default
p: (0,0)
a: {(0,0), (1,1)}
hello
```

The operators on references to objects are:

- Field access, using either a qualified name or a field access expression
- Method invocation
- The cast operator

  The string concatenation operator + which, when given a **String** operand and a reference, will convert the reference to a **String** by invoking the **to String** method of the referenced object (using **"null"** if either the reference or the result of **to String** is a null reference), and then will produce a newly created **String** that is the concatenation of the two strings
- The `instanceof` operator

- The reference equality operators `==` and `!=`
- The conditional operator `?:`.

There may be many references to the same object. Most objects have state, stored in the fields of objects that are instances of classes or in the variables that are the components of an array object.

If two variables contain references to the same object, the state of the object can be modified using one variable's reference to the object, and then the altered state can be observed through the reference in the other variable.

The example program:

```
class Value {int val;}
class Test {
    public static void main(String[] args) {
        int i1 = 3;
        int i2 = i1;
        i2 = 4;
        System.out.print("i1==" + i1);
        System.out.println(" but i2==" + i2);
        Value v1 = new Value();
        v1.val = 5;
        Value v2 = v1;
        v2.val = 6;
        System.out.print("v1.val==" +
    v1.val);
        System.out.println(" and v2.val==" +
    v2.val);
    }
}
```

produces the output:

```
i1==3 but i2==4
v1.val==6 and v2.val==6
```

because `v1.val` and `v2.val` reference the same instance variable in the one `Value` object created by the only `new` expression, while `i1` and `i2` are different variables.

See and for examples of the creation and use of arrays. Each object has an associated lock, which is used by `synchronized` methods and the `synchronized` statement to provide control over concurrent access to state by multiple threads.

THE CLASS OBJECT

The class **Object** is a superclass of all other classes. A variable of type **Object** can hold a reference to the null reference or to any object, whether it is an instance of a class or an array All class and array types inherit the methods of class **Object**, which are summarized here:

```
package java.lang;
public class Object {
    public final Class<?> getClass() {...}
    public String toString() {...}
    public boolean equals(Object obj) {...}
    public int hashCode() {...}
    protected Object clone()
        throws CloneNotSupportedException
    {...}
    public final void wait()
        throws IllegalMonitorStateException,
        InterruptedException {...}
public final void wait(long millis)
    throws IllegalMonitorStateException,
            InterruptedException {...}
public final void wait(long millis, int nanos)
{...}
        throws IllegalMonitorStateException,
            InterruptedException {...}
public final void notify() {...}
        throws IllegalMonitorStateException
    public final void notifyAll() {...}
        throws IllegalMonitorStateException
protected void finalize()
        throws Throwable {...}
}
```

The members of **Object** are as follows:

- The method getClass returns the Class object that represents the class of the object. A Class object exists for each reference type. It can be used, for example, to discover the fully qualified name of a class, its members, its immediate superclass, and any interfaces that it implements. A class method that is declared synchronized synchronizes on the lock associated with the Class object of the class. The method Object.getClass() must be treated specially by a Java compiler. The type of a method invocation e.getClass(), where the expression e has the static type T, is Class<? extends |T|>.

- The method toString returns a String representation of the object.
- The methods equals and hashCode are very useful in hashtables such as java.util.Hashtable. The method equals defines a notion of object equality, which is based on value, not reference, comparison.
- The method clone is used to make a duplicate of an object.
- The methods wait, notify, and notifyAll are used in concurrent programming using threads, as described in.
- The method finalize is run just before an object is destroyed and is described in.

THE CLASS STRING

Instances of class `String` represent sequences of Unicode characters. A `String` object has a constant (unchanging) value. String literals are references to instances of class `String`.

The string concatenation operator `+` implicitly creates a new `String` object when the result is not a compile-time constant.

WHEN REFERENCE TYPES ARE THE SAME

Two reference types are the *same compile-time type* if they have the same binary name and their type parametres, if any, are the same, applying this definition recursively. When two reference types are the same, they are sometimes said to be the *same class* or the *same interface.*

At run time, several reference types with the same binary name may be loaded simultaneously by different class loaders. These types may or may not represent the same type declaration. Even if two such types do represent the same type declaration, they are considered distinct.

Two reference types are the *same run-time type* if:

- They are both class or both interface types, are defined by the same class loader, and have the same binary name, in which case they are sometimes said to be the *same run-time class* or the *same run-time interface.*
- They are both array types, and their component types are the same run-time type.

TYPE VARIABLES

A type variable is an unqualified identifier. Type variables are introduced by generic class declarations generic interface declarations generic method declarations and by generic constructor declarations.

```
    TypeParameter:
        TypeVariable TypeBoundopt
    TypeBound:
    extends ClassOrInterfaceType
AdditionalBoundListopt
    AdditionalBoundList:
        AdditionalBound AdditionalBoundList
        AdditionalBound
    AdditionalBound:
        & InterfaceType
```

Type variables have an optional bound, T & $I_1 ... I_n$. The bound consists of either a type variable, or a class or interface type T possibly followed by further interface types $I_1 ,..., I_n$. If no bound is given for a type variable, `Object` is assumed. It is a compile-time error if any of the types $I_1 ... I_n$ is a class type or type variable.

The erasures of all constituent types of a bound must be pairwise different, or a compile-time error occurs. The order of types in a bound is only significant in that the erasure of a type variable is determined by the first type in its bound, and that a class type or type variable may only appear in the first position. A type variable may not at the same time be a subtype of two interface types which are different parametreizations of the same generic interface. The members of a type variable X with bound $T \& I_1 ... I_n$ are the members of the intersection type $T \& I_1 ... I_n$ appearing at the point where the type variable is declared.

Discussion: The following example illustrates what members a type variable has.

```
package TypeVarMembers;
    class C {
          void mCDefault() {}
          public void mCPublic() {}
          private void mCPrivate() {}
          protected void mCProtected() {}
    }
    class CT extends C implements I {}
    interface I {
          void mI();}
          <T extends C & I> void test(T t) {
                t.mI();// OK
                t.mCDefault();// OK
                t.mCPublic();// OK
                t.mCPrivate();// compile-time
    error
                t.mCProtected();// OK
          }
    }
```

The type variable T has the same members as the intersection type C & I, which in turn has the same members as the empty class CT, defined in the same scope with equivalent supertypes. The members of an interface are always public, and therefore always inherited (unless overridden). Hence mI is a member of CT and of T. Among the members of C, all but mCPrivate are inherited by CT, and are therefore members of both CT and T. If C had been declared in a different package than T, then the call to mCDefault would give rise to a compile-time error, as that member would not be accessible at the point where T is declared.

PARAMETREIZED TYPES

A parametreized type consists of a class or interface name C and an actual type argument list <T_1 ,..., T_n>. It is a compile time error if C is not the name of a generic class or interface, or if the number of type arguments in the actual type argument list differs from the number of declared type parametres of C. In the following, whenever we speak of a class or interface type, we include the generic version as well, unless explicitly excluded.

Throughout this section, let A_1 ,..., A_n be the formal type parametres of C, and let be B_i be the declared bound of A_i. The notation $[A_i := T_i]$ denotes substitution of the type variable A_i with the type T_i, for $1 \leq i \leq n$, and is used throughout this specification. Let $P = G<T_1,..., T_n>$ be a parametreized type. It must be the case that, after *P* is subjected to capture conversion resulting in the type *G*<*X1*,..., *Xn*>, for each actual type argument X_i, $1 \leq i \leq n$, $X_i <: B_i[A_1 := X_1,..., A_n := X_n]$, or a compile time error occurs.

```
Example: Parameterized types.
Vector<String>
Seq<Seq<A>>
Seq<String>.Zipper<Integer>
Collection<Integer>
Pair<String,String>
// Vector<int> – illegal, primitive types
cannot be arguments
// Pair<String> – illegal, not enough
arguments
// Pair<String,String,String> – illegal, too
many arguments
```

Two parametreized types are provably distinct if either of the following conditions hold:

- They are invocations of distinct generic type declarations.
- Any of their type arguments are provably distinct.

TYPE ARGUMENTS AND WILDCARDS

Type arguments may be either reference types or wildcards.

```
TypeArguments:
    < ActualTypeArgumentList >
ActualTypeArgumentList:
    ActualTypeArgument
ActualTypeArgumentList, ActualTypeArgument
    ActualTypeArgument:
ReferenceType
Wildcard
Wildcard:
? WildcardBoundsOpt
WildcardBounds:
extends ReferenceType
super ReferenceType
Discussion:
Examples:
    void printCollection(Collection<?> c) {/
    / a     wildcard collection
    for (Object o: c) {
    System.out.println(o);
    }
    }
```

Note that using Collection<Object> as the type of the incoming parametre, c, would not be nearly as useful; the method could only be used with an actual parametre that had type Collection<Object>, which would be quite rare. In contrast, the use of an unbounded wildcard allows any kind of collection to be used as a parametre. Wildcards are useful in situations where only partial knowledge about the type parametre is required.

Discussion: Example - Wildcard parametreized types as component types of array types.

```
public Method getMethod(Class<?>[]
parametreTypes) {... }
```

Wildcards may be given explicit bounds, just like regular type variable declarations. An upper bound is signified by the syntax:

```
? extends B
```

, where *B* is the bound.

Discussion

Example: Bounded wildcards.

```
boolean addAll(Collection<? extends E> c)
```

Here, the method is declared within the interface Collection<E>, and is designed to add all the elements of its incoming argument to the collection upon which it is invoked. A natural tendency would be to use Collection<E> as the type of c, but this is unnecessarily restrictive. An alternative would be to declare the method itself to be generic:

```
<T> boolean addAll(Collection<T> c)
```

This version is sufficiently flexible, but note that the type parametre is used only once in the signature. This reflects the fact that the type parametre is not being used to express any kind of interdependency between the type(s) of the argument(s), the return type and/or throws type. In the absence of such interdependency, generic methods are considered bad style, and wildcards are preferred. Unlike ordinary type variables declared in a method signature, no type inference is required when using a wildcard. Consequently, it is permissible to declare lower bounds on a wildcard, using the syntax:

```
? super B
```

, where *B* is a lower bound.

Discussion

Example: Lower bounds on wildcards.

```
Reference(T referent, ReferenceQueue<? super
T> queue);
```

Here, the referent can be inserted into any queue whose element type is a super type of the type T of the referent. Two type arguments are provably distinct if neither of the arguments is a type variable or wildcard, and the two arguments are not the same type.

Discussion: The relationship of wildcards to established type theory is an interesting one, which we briefly allude to here. Wildcards are a restricted form of existential types. Given a generic type declaration *G<T extends B>*, *G<?>* is roughly analogous to *Some X <: B. G<X>*. Readers interested in a more comprehensive discussion should refer to *On Variance-Based Subtyping for Parametric Types* by Atsushi Igarashi and Mirko Viroli, in the proceedings of the 16th European Conference on Object Oriented Programming (ECOOP 2002).

Wildcards differ in certain details from the constructs described in the aforementioned paper, in particular in the use of capture conversion ratther than the close operation described by Igarashi and Viroli. For a formal account of wildcards, see *Wild FJ* by Mads Torgersen, Erik Ernst and Christian Plesner Hansen, in the 12th workshop on Foundations of Object Oriented Programming (FOOL 2005). Historically, wildcards are a direct descendant of the work by Atsushi Igarashi and Mirko Viroli.

This work itself builds upon earlier work by Kresten Thorup and Mads Torgersen ("Unifying Genericity", ECOOP 99), as well as a long tradition of work on declaration based variance that goes back to Pierre America's work on POOL (OOPSLA 89)

TYPE ARGUMENT CONTAINMENT AND EQUIVALENCE

A type argument TA_1 is said to contain another type argument TA_2, written $TA_2 <= TA_1$, if the set of types denoted by TA_2 is provably a subset of the set of types denoted by TA_1 under the following rules (where <: denotes subtyping:

- ? extends T <= ? extends S if *T <: S*
- ? super T <= ? super S if *S <: T*
- T <= T
- T <= ? extends T
- T <= ? super T

MEMBERS AND CONSTRUCTORS OF PARAMETERIZED TYPES

Let C be a class or interface declaration with formal type parameters $A_1...,A_n$, and let $C<T_1...,T_n>$ be an invocation of C, where, for $1 \leq i \leq n$, T_i are types (rather than wildcards).

Then:

- Let *m* be a member or constructor declaration in *C*, whose type as declared is *T*. Then the type of *m* in the type $C<T_1...,T_n>$, is $T[A_1:= T_1..., A_n:= T_n]$.
- Let *m* be a member or constructor declaration in *D*, where *D* is a class extended by *C* or an interface implemented by *C*. Let $D<U_1...,U_k>$ be the supertype of $C<T_1...,T_n>$ that corresponds to *D*. Then the type of *m* in $C<T_1...,T_n>$ is the type of *m* in $D<U_1...,U_k>$.

If any of the type arguments to a parameterized type are wildcards, the type of its members and constructors is undefined.

Discussion: This is of no consequence, as it is impossible to access a member of a parameterized type without performing capture conversion, and it is impossible to use a wildcard type after the keyword new in a class instance creation expression

TYPE ERASURE

Type erasure is a mapping from types (possibly including parameterized types and type variables) to types (that are never parameterized types or type variables). We write $|T|$ for the erasure of type *T*. The erasure mapping is defined as follows.

- The erasure of a parameterized type $G<T_1...,T_n>$ is $|G|$.
- The erasure of a nested type *T.C* is $|T|.C$.
- The erasure of an array type *T[]* is $|T|[]$.
- The erasure of a type variable is the erasure of its leftmost bound.
- The erasure of every other type is the type itself.

The erasure of a method signature *s* is a signature consisting of the same name as *s*, and the erasures of all the formal parameter types given in *s*.

REIFIABLE TYPES

Because some type information is erased during compilation, not all types are available at run time. Types that are completely available at run time are known as *reifiable types*. A type is reifiable if and only if one of the following holds:

- It refers to a non-generic type declaration.
- It is a parameterized type in which all type arguments are unbounded wildcards.
- It is a raw type.
- It is a primitive type.
- It is an array type whose component type is reifiable.

Discussion: The decision not to make all generic types reifiable is one of the most crucial, and controversial design decisions involving the language's type system.

Ultimately, the most important motivation for this decision is compatibility with existing code. Naively, the addition of new constructs such as genericity has no implications for pre-existing code.

The programming language per se, is compatible with earlier versions as long as every program written in the previous versions retains its meaning in the new version. However, this notion, which may be termed language compatibility, is of purely theoretical interest.

Real programs (even trivial ones, such as "Hello World") are composed of several compilation units, some of which are provided by the Java platform (such as elements of **java.lang** or **java.util**).

In practice then, the minimum requirement is platform compatibillity - that any program written for the prior version of the platform continues to function unchanged in the new platform. One way to provide platform compatibillity is to leave existing platform functionality unchanged, only adding new functionality.

For example, rather than modify the existing Collections hierarchy in **java.util**, one might introduce a new library utilizing genericity. The disadvantages of such a scheme is that it is extremely difficult for pre-existing clients of the Collection library to migrate to the new library. Collections are used to exchange data between independently developed modules; if a vendor decides to switch to the new, generic, library, that vendor must also distribute two versions of their code, to be compatible with their clients. Libraries that are dependent on other vendors code cannot be modified to use genericity until the supplier's library is updated. If two modules are mutually dependent, the changes must be made simultaneously.

Clearly, platform compatibility, as outlined above, does not provide a realistic path for adoption of a pervasive new feature such as genericity. Therefore, the design of the generic type system seeks to support migration compatibility. Migration compatibiliy allows the evolution of existing code to take advantage of generics without imposing dependencies between independently developed software modules. The price of migration compatibility is that a full and sound reification of the generic type system is not possible, at least while the migration is taking place.

RAW TYPES

To facilitate interfacing with non-generic legacy code, it is also possible to use as a type the erasure of a parameterized type. Such a type is called a *raw type*.

More precisely, a raw type is define to be either:

- The name of a generic type declaration used without any accompanying actual type parameters.
- Any non-static type member of a raw type *R* that is not inherited from a superclass or superinterface of *R*.

Discussion: The latter point may not be immediately self evident. Presenting for your consideration, then, the following example:

```
class Outer<T>{
    T t;
    class Inner {
    T setOuterT(T t1) {t = t1;return t;}
    }
}
```

The type of the member(s) of **Inner** depends on the type parameter of **Outer**. If **Outer** is raw, **Inner** must be treated as raw as well, as their is no valid binding for **T**. This rule applies only to type members that are not inherited. Inherited type members that depend on type variables will be inherited as raw types as a consequence of the rule that the supertypes of a raw type are erased, described later in this section.

Discussion: Another implication of the rules above is that a generic inner class of a raw type can itself only be used as a raw type:

```
class Outer<T>{
    class Inner<S> {
        S s;
    }
}
 it is not possible to access Inner as
partially raw type (a "rare" type)
Outer.Inner<Double> x = null;// illegal
Double d = x.s;
```

because **Outer** itself is raw, so are all its inner classes, including **Inner**, and so it is not possible to pass any type parameters to it. The use of raw types is allowed only as a concession to compatibility of legacy code.

The use of raw types in code written after the introduction of genericity into the Java programming language is strongly discouraged. It is possible that future versions of the Java programming language will disallow the use of raw types. It is a compile-time error to attempt to use a type member of a parameterized type as a raw type.

Discussion: This means that the ban on "rare" types extends to the case where the qualifying type is parameterized, but we attempt to use the inner class as a raw type:

```
Outer<Integer>.Inner x = null;// illegal
```

This is the opposite of the case we discussed above. There is no practical justification for this half baked type. In legacy code, no type parameters are used. In non-legacy code, we should use the generic types correctly and pass all the required actual type parameters.

Discussion: Variables of a raw type can be assigned from values of any of the type's parametric instances. For instance, it is possible to assign a **Vector<String>** to a **Vector**, based on the subtyping rules. The reverse assignment from **Vector** to **Vector<String>** is unsafe (since the raw vector might have had a different element type), but is still permitted using unchecked conversion in order to enable interfacing with legacy code. In this case, a compiler will issue an unchecked warning. The superclasses (respectively, superinterfaces) of a raw type are the erasures of the superclasses (superinterfaces) of any of its parameterized invocations.

The type of a constructor, instance method, or non-static field *M* of a raw type *C* that is not inherited from its superclasses or superinterfaces is the erasure of its type in the generic declaration corresponding to *C*. The type of a static member of a raw type *C* is the same as its type in the generic declaration corresponding to *C*.

It is a compile-time error to pass actual type parameters to a non-static type member of a raw type that is not inherited from its superclasses or superinterfaces. To make sure that potential violations of the typing rules are always flagged, some accesses to members of a raw type will result in warning messages. The rules for generating warnings when accessing members or constructors of raw types are as follows:

- An invocation of a method or constructor of a raw type generates an unchecked warning if erasure changes any of the types of any of the arguments to the method or constructor.
- An assignment to a field of a raw type generates an unchecked warning if erasure changes the field's type.

No unchecked warning is required for a method call when the argument types do not change (even if the result type and/or throws clause changes), for reading from a field, or for a class instance creation of a raw type. The supertype of a class may be a raw type. Member accesses for the class are treated as normal, and member accesses for the supertype are treated as for raw types. In the constructor of the class, calls to super are treated as method calls on a raw type.

Discussion:

```
Example: Raw types.
class Cell<E>
   E value;
```

```
        Cell (E v) {value=v;}
        A get() {return value;}
        void set(E v) {value=v;}
    }
    Cell x = new Cell<String>("abc");
    x.value;// OK, has type Object
    x.get();// OK, has type Object
    x.set("def");// unchecked warning
```

Discussion:

For example,

```
    import java.util.*;
    class NonGeneric {
        Collection<Number> myNumbers(){return
null;}
    }
    abstract class RawMembers<T> extends
NonGeneric implements Collection<String> {
        static Collection<NonGeneric> cng =
    new ArrayList<NonGeneric>();
        public static void main(String[] args) {
            RawMembers rw = null;
            Collection<Number> cn =
rw.myNumbers();// ok
            Iterator<String> is = rw.iterator();/
    / unchecked warning
            Collection<NonGeneric> cnn = rw.cng;/
    / ok - static member
        }
    }
    RawMembers<T> inherits the method
    Iterator<String> iterator()
```

from the **Collection<String>** superinterface. However, the type **RawMembers** inherits **iterator()** from the erasure of its superinterface, which means that the return type of the member **iterator()** is the erasure of **Iterator<<String>, Iterator**. As a result, the attempt to assign to **rw.iterator()** requires an unchecked conversion from **Iterator** to **Iterator<String>**, causing an unchecked warning to be issued. In contrast, the static member **cng** retains its full parameterized type even when accessed through a object of raw type (note that access to a static member through an instance is considered bad style and is to be discouraged). The member **myNumbers** is inherited from the **NonGeneric** (whose erasure is also **NonGeneric**) and so retains its full parameterized type.

Discussion: Raw types are closly related to wildcards. Both are based on existential types. Raw types can be thought of as wildcards whose type rules are deliberately unsound, to accommodate interaction with legacy code.

Historically, raw types preceded wildcards; they were first introduced in GJ, and described in the paper *Making the future safe for the past: Adding Genericity to the Java Programming Language* by Gilad Bracha, Martin Odersky, David Stoutamire, and Philip Wadler, in Proc. of the ACM Conf. on Object-Oriented Programming, Systems, Languages and Applications, (OOPSLA 98) October 1998.

INTERSECTION TYPES

An intersection type takes the form T_1 &... & T_n, $n>0$, where T_i, $1 \leq i \leq n$, are type expressions. Intersection types arise in the processes of capture conversion and type inference.It is not possible to write an intersection type directly as part of a program; no syntax supports this. The values of an intersection type are those objects that are values of all of the types T_i, for $1 \leq i \leq n$.

The members of an intersection type T_1 &... & T_n are determined as follows:

- For each T_i, $1 \leq i \leq n$, let C_i be the most specific class or array type such that T_i <: C_i Then there must be some T_k <: C_k such that C_k <: C_i for any i, $1 \leq i \leq n$, or a compile-time error occurs.
- For $1 \leq j \leq n$, if T_j is a type variable, then let IT_j be an interface whose members are the same as the public members of T_j; otherwise, if T_j is an interface, then let IT_j be T_j.
- Then the intersection type has the same members as a class type with an empty body, direct superclass

C_k and direct superinterfaces $IT_1..., IT_n$, declared in the same package in which the intersection type appears.

Discussion: It is worth dwelling upon the distinction between intersection types and the bounds of type variables. Every type variable bound induces an intersection type. This intersection type is often trivial (i.e., consists of a single type).

The form of a bound is restricted (only the first element may be a class or type variable, and only one type variable may appear in the bound) to preclude certain awkward situations coming into existence. However, capture conversion can lead to the creation of type variables whose bounds are more general (e.g., array types).

SUBTYPING

The subtype and supertype relations are binary relations on types. The *supertypes* of a type are obtained by reflexive and transitive closure over the direct supertype relation, written $S >_1 T$, which is defined by rules given later in this section. We write $S :> T$ to indicate that the supertype relation holds between S and T. S is a proper supertype of T, written $T < S$, if $S :> T$ and $S \neq T$. The *subtypes* of a type T are all types U such that T is a supertype of U, and the null type. We write $T <: S$ to indicate that that the subtype relation holds between types T and S. T is a *proper subtype* of S, written $T < S$, if $T <: S$ and $S \neq T$. T is a *direct subtype* of S, written $T <_1 S$, if $S >_1 T$.

Subtyping does not extend through generic types: $T <: U$ does not imply that $C<T> <: C<U>$.

SUBTYPING AMONG PRIMITIVE TYPES

The following rules define the direct supertype relation among the primitive types:

double $>_1$ float

float $>_1$ long

long $>_1$ int

int $>_1$ char

int $>_1$ short

short $>_1$ byte

SUBTYPING AMONG CLASS AND INTERFACE TYPES

Let C be a type declaration with zero or more type parameters $F_1..., F_n$ which have corresponding bounds $B_1..., B_n$. That type declaration defines a set of parameterized types $C_2 <T_1...,T_n>$, where each argument type T_i ranges over all types that are subtypes of all types listed in the corresponding bound. That is, for each bound type S_i in B_i, T_i is a subtype of $S_i[F_1{:=}\ T_1..., F_n{:=}\ T_n]$.

Given a type declaration for $C<F_1...,F_n>$, the *direct supertypes* of the parameterized type $C<F_1...,F_n>$ are all of the following:

- The direct superclasses of C.
- The direct superinterfaces of C.
- The type Object, if C is an interface type with no direct superinterfaces.
- The raw type C.
- The direct supertypes of the type $C<T_1...,T_n>$, where $T_i, 1 \leq i \leq n$, is a type, are $D<U_1$ *theta...*, U_k *theta*$>$, where
- $D<U_1...,U_k>$ is a direct supertype of $C<F_1...,F_n>$, and *theta* is the substitution $[F_1{:=}\ T_1..., F_n{:=}\ T_n]$.
- $C<S_1...,S_n>$ where S_i contains T_i for $1 \leq i \leq n$.

The direct supertypes of the type $C<R_1...,R_n>$, where at least one of the R_i, $1 \leq i \leq n$, is a wildcard type argument, are the direct supertypes of $C<X_1...,X_n>$, where $C<X_1...,X_n>$ is the result of applying capture conversion to $C<R_1...,R_n>$. The direct supertypes of an intersection type T_1 &... & T_n, are T_i, $1 \leq i \leq n$. The direct supertypes of a type variable are the types listed in its bound.

The direct supertypes of the null type are all reference types other than the null type itself. In addition to the above rules, a type variable is a direct supertype of its lower bound.

SUBTYPING AMONG ARRAY TYPES

The following rules define the direct subtype relation among array types:

- If S and T are both reference types, then $S[] >_1 T[]$ iff $S >_1 T$.
- Object $>_1$ Object[]

- Cloneable $>_1$ Object[]
- java.io.Serializable $>_1$ Object[]
- If *p* is a primitive type, then:
  - Object $>_1$ p[]
  - Cloneable $>_1$ p[]
  - java.io.Serializable $>_1$ p[]

WHERE TYPES ARE USED

Types are used when they appear in declarations or in certain expressions. The following code fragment contains one or more instances of most kinds of usage of a type:

```
import java.util.Random;
class MiscMath<T extends Number>{
   int divisor;
   MiscMath(int divisor) {
        this.divisor = divisor;
   }
   float ratio(long l) {
        try {
             l/= divisor;
        } catch (Exception e) {
        if (e instanceof ArithmeticException)
                  l = Long.MAX_VALUE;
             else
                  l = 0;
        }
             return (float)l;
        }
        double gausser() {
             Random r = new Random();
             double[] val = new double[2];
             val[0] = r.nextGaussian();
             val[1] = r.nextGaussian();
             return (val[0] + val[1])/ 2;
}
Collection<Number> fromArray(Number[] na) {
        Collection<Number> cn = new
   ArrayList<Number>();
```

```
            for (Number n: na) {
                    cn.add(n)
}
return cn;
}
    void <S> loop(S s){this.<S>loop(s);}
}
```

In this example, types are used in declarations of the following:

- Imported types; here the type Random, imported from the type java.util.Random of the package java.util, is declared
- Fields, which are the class variables and instance variables of classes, and constants of interfaces; here the field divisor in the class MiscMath is declared to be of type int
- Method parameters; here the parameter l of the method ratio is declared to be of type long
- Method results; here the result of the method ratio is declared to be of type float, and the result of the method gausser is declared to be of type double
- Constructor parameters; here the parameter of the constructor for MiscMath is declared to be of type int
- Local variables the local variables r and val of the method gausser are declared to be of types Random and double[] (array of double)
- Exception handler parameters here the exception handler parameter e of the catch clause is declared to be of type Exception
- Type variables; here the type variable T has Number as its declared bound.

In expressions of the following kinds:

- Class instance creations; here a local variable r of method gausser is initialized by a class instance creation expression that uses the type Random
- Generic class instance creations here Number is used as a type argument in the expression new ArrayList<Number>()
- Array creations here the local variable val of method

gausser is initialized by an array creation expression that creates an array of double with size 2.

- Generic method or constructor invocations here the method loop calls itself with an explicit type argument S.
- Casts; here the return statement of the method ratio uses the float type in a cast.
- The instanceof operator here the instanceof operator tests whether e is assignment compatible with the type ArithmeticException.

Types are also used as arguments to parameterized types; here the type Number is used as an argument in the parameterized type Collection<Number>.

VARIABLES

A variable is a storage location and has an associated type, sometimes called its *compile-time type*, that is either a primitive type or a reference type. A variable's value is changed by an assignment or by a prefix or postfix ++ (increment) or — (decrement) operator.

Compatibility of the value of a variable with its type is guaranteed by the design of the Java programming language, as long as a program does not give rise to unchecked warnings. Default values are compatible and all assignments to a variable are checked for assignment compatibility, usually at compile time, but, in a single case involving arrays, a run-time check is made.

VARIABLES OF PRIMITIVE TYPE

A variable of a primitive type always holds a value of that exact primitive type.

VARIABLES OF REFERENCE TYPE

A variable of a class type *T* can hold a null reference or a reference to an instance of class *T* or of any class that is a subclass of *T*. A variable of an interface type can hold a null reference or a reference to any instance of any class that implements the interface. Discussion: Note that a variable is not guaranteed to always refer to a subtype of its declared type, but only to subclasses or subinterfaces of the declared type. This is due to the possibility of heap pollution discussed below. If *T* is a primitive type, then a variable of type "array of *T*" can hold a null reference or a reference to any array of type "array of *T*"; if *T* is a reference type, then a variable of type "array of *T*" can hold a null reference or a reference to any array of type "array of *S*" such that type *S* is a subclass or subinterface of type *T*.

In addition, a variable of type **Object[]** can hold an array of any reference type. A variable of type **Object** can hold a null reference or a reference to any object, whether class instance or array.

HEAP POLLUTION

It is possible that a variable of a parameterized type refers to an object that is not of that parameterized type. This situation is known as heap pollution. This situation can only occur if the program performed some operation that would give rise to an unchecked warning at compile-time.

Discussion: For example, the code:

```
List l = new ArrayList<Number>();
List<String> ls = l;// unchecked warning
```

gives rise to an unchecked warning, because it is not possible to ascertain, either at compile-time (within the limits of the compile-time type checking rules) or at run-time, whether the variable l does indeed refer to a **List<String>**. If the code above is executed, heap pollution arises, as the variable ls, declared to be a **List<String>**, refers to a value that is not in fact a **List<String>**.

The problem cannot be identified at run-time because type variables are not reified, and thus instances do not carry any information at run-time regarding the actual type parameters used to create them. In a simple example as given above, it may appear that it should be straightforward to identify the situation at compile-time and give a compilation error. However, in the general (and typical) case, the value of the variable l may be the result of an invocation of a separately compiled method, or its value may depend upon arbitrary control flow. The code above is therefore very atypical, and indeed very bad style. Assignment from a value of a raw type to a variable of a parameterized type should only be used when combining legacy code which does not make use of parameterized types with more modern code that does.

If no operation that requires an unchecked warning to be issued takes place, heap pollution cannot occur. Note that this does not imply that heap pollution only occurs if an unchecked warning actually occurred. It is possible to run a program where some of the binaries were compiled by a compiler for an older version of the Java programming language, or by a compiler that allows the unchecked warnings to suppressed. This practice is unhealthy at best. Conversely, it is possible that despite executing code that could (and perhaps did) give rise to an unchecked warning, no heap pollution takes place. Indeed, good programming practice requires that the programmer satisfy herself that despite any unchecked warning, the code is correct and heap pollution will not occur. The variable will always refer to an object that is an instance of a class that implements the parameterized type.

Discussion: For instance, the value of l in the example above is always a **List**.

KINDS OF VARIABLES

There are seven kinds of variables:

1. A *class variable* is a field declared using the keyword static within a class declaration, or with or without the keyword static within an interface declaration. A class variable is created when its class or interface is prepared and is initialized to a default value. The class variable effectively ceases to exist when its class or interface is unloaded.
2. An *instance variable* is a field declared within a class declaration without using the keyword static. If a class *T* has a field *a* that is an instance variable, then a new instance variable *a* is created and initialized to a default value as part of each newly created object

of class *T* or of any class that is a subclass of *T*. The instance variable effectively ceases to exist when the object of which it is a field is no longer referenced, after any necessary finalization of the object has been completed.

3. *Array components* are unnamed variables that are created and initialized to default values whenever a new object that is an array is created. The array components effectively cease to exist when the array is no longer referenced. for a description of arrays.
4. *Method parameters* name argument values passed to a method. For every parameter declared in a method declaration, a new parameter variable is created each time that method is invoked. The new variable is initialized with the corresponding argument value from the method invocation. The method parameter effectively ceases to exist when the execution of the body of the method is complete.
5. *Constructor parameters* name argument values passed to a constructor. For every parameter declared in a constructor declaration, a new parameter variable is created each time a class instance creation expression or explicit constructor invocation invokes that constructor. The new variable is initialized with the corresponding argument value from the creation expression or constructor invocation. The constructor parameter effectively ceases to exist when the execution of the body of the constructor is complete.
6. An *exception-handler parameter* is created each time an exception is caught by a catch clause of a try statement. The new variable is initialized with the actual object associated with the exception The exception-handler parameter effectively ceases to exist when execution of the block associated with the catch clause is complete.
7. *Local variables* are declared by local variable declaration statements. Whenever the flow of control enters a block or for statement, a new variable is

created for each local variable declared in a local variable declaration statement immediately contained within that block or for statement. A local variable declaration statement may contain an expression which initializes the variable. The local variable with an initializing expression is not initialized, however, until the local variable declaration statement that declares it is executed. (The rules of definite assignment prevent the value of a local variable from being used before it has been initialized or otherwise assigned a value.) The local variable effectively ceases to exist when the execution of the block or for statement is complete.

Were it not for one exceptional situation, a local variable could always be regarded as being created when its local variable declaration statement is executed. The exceptional situation involves the **switch** statement, where it is possible for control to enter a block but bypass execution of a local variable declaration statement.

Because of the restrictions imposed by the rules of definite assignment, however, the local variable declared by such a bypassed local variable declaration statement cannot be used before it has been definitely assigned a value by an assignment expression.

The following example contains several different kinds of variables:

```
class Point {
    static int numPoints;// numPoints is a
class variable
int x, y;// x and y are instance variables
    int[] w = new int[10];// w[0] is an array
      component
    int setX(int x) {// x is a method
    parameter
    int oldx = this.x;// oldx is a local
    variable
    this.x = x;
    return oldx;
```

```
    }
}
```

FINAL VARIABLES

A variable can be declared **final**. A final variable may only be assigned to once. It is a compile time error if a final variable is assigned to unless it is definitely unassigned immediately prior to the assignment. A blank final is a final variable whose declaration lacks an initializer.

Once a **final** variable has been assigned, it always contains the same value. If a **final** variable holds a reference to an object, then the state of the object may be changed by operations on the object, but the variable will always refer to the same object. This applies also to arrays, because arrays are objects; if a **final** variable holds a reference to an array, then the components of the array may be changed by operations on the array, but the variable will always refer to the same array.

Declaring a variable **final** can serve as useful documentation that its value will not change and can help avoid programming errors.

In the example:

```
class Point {
    int x, y;
    int useCount;
    Point(int x, int y) {this.x = x; this.y
    = y;}
    final static Point origin = new Point(0,
    0);
}
```

the class **Point** declares a final class variable **origin**. The **origin** variable holds a reference to an object that is an instance of class **Point** whose coordinates are (0, 0). The value of the variable **Point.origin** can never change, so it always refers to the same **Point** object, the one created by its initializer. However, an operation on this **Point** object might change its state-for example, modifying its **useCount** or even, misleadingly, its x or y coordinate. We call a variable, of primitive type or type **String**, that is final and initialized with a compile-time constant expression a *constant variable*. Whether a variable is a constant variable or not may have implications with respect to class initialization, binary compatibility and definite assignment.

INITIAL VALUES OF VARIABLES

Every variable in a program must have a value before its value is used:

- Each class variable, instance variable, or array component is initialized with a *default value* when it is created:
  - For type byte, the default value is zero, that is, the value of (byte)0.
  - For type short, the default value is zero, that is, the value of (short)0.
  - For type int, the default value is zero, that is, 0.
  - For type long, the default value is zero, that is, 0L.
  - For type float, the default value is positive zero, that is, 0.0f.
  - For type double, the default value is positive zero, that is, 0.0d.
  - For type char, the default value is the null character, that is, '\u0000'.
  - For type boolean, the default value is false.
  - For all reference types, the default value is null.
- Each method parameter is initialized to the corresponding argument value provided by the invoker of the method.
- Each constructor parameter is initialized to the corresponding argument value provided by a class instance creation expression or explicit constructor invocation.
- An exception-handler parameter is initialized to the thrown object representing the exception.
- A local variable must be explicitly given a value before it is used, by either initialization or assignment, in a way that can be verified by the compiler using the rules for definite assignment.

The example program:

```
class Point {
    static int npoints;
    int x, y;
    Point root;
}
class Test {
    public static void main(String[] args) {
        System.out.println("npoints=" +
    Point.npoints);
        Point p = new Point();
        System.out.println("p.x=" + p.x + ",
    p.y=" + p.y);
        System.out.println("p.root=" +
    p.root);
    }
}
prints:
npoints=0
p.x=0, p.y=0
p.root=null
```

illustrating the default initialization of npoints, which occurs when the class Point is prepared, and the default initialization of x, y, and root, which occurs when a new Point is instantiated. A full description of all aspects of loading, linking, and initialization of classes and interfaces, plus a description of the instantiation of classes to make new class instances.

TYPES, CLASSES, AND INTERFACES

In the Java programming language, every variable and every expression has a type that can be determined at compile time. The type may be a primitive type or a reference type. Reference types include class types and interface types. Reference types are introduced by type declarations, which include class declarations and interface declarations. We often use the term *type* to refer to either a class or an interface. Every object belongs to some particular class: the class that was mentioned in the creation expression that produced the object, the class whose **Class** object was used to invoke a reflective method to produce the object, or the **String** class for objects implicitly created by the string concatenation operator +.

This class is called the *class of the object*. (Arrays also have a class, as described at the end of this section.) An object is said to be an instance of its class and of all superclasses of its class. Sometimes a variable or expression is said to have a "run-time type". This refers to the class of the object referred to by the value of the variable or expression at run time, assuming that the value is not **null**. The compile time type of a variable is always declared, and the compile time type of an expression can be deduced at compile time. The compile time type limits the possible values that the variable can hold or the expression can produce at run time. If a run-time value is a reference that is not **null**, it refers to an object or array that has a class, and that class will necessarily be compatible with the compile-time type. Even though a variable or expression may have a compile-time type that is an interface type, there are no instances of interfaces. A variable or expression whose type is an interface type can reference any object whose class implements that interface. Here is an example of creating new objects and of the distinction between the type of a variable and the class of an object:

```
public interface Colorable {
    void setColor(byte r, byte g, byte b);
}
class Point {int x, y;}
class ColoredPoint extends Point implements
    Colorable {
    byte r, g, b;
    public void setColor(byte rv, byte gv, byte
    bv) {
        r = rv; g = gv; b = bv;
    }
}
class Test {
    public static void main(String[] args) {
        Point p = new Point();
```

```
        ColoredPoint cp = new ColoredPoint();
        p = cp;
Colorable c = cp;
}
}
```

In this example:

- The local variable p of the method main of class Test has type Point and is initially assigned a reference to a new instance of class Point.
- The local variable cp similarly has as its type ColoredPoint, and is initially assigned a reference to a new instance of class ColoredPoint.
- The assignment of the value of cp to the variable p causes p to hold a reference to a ColoredPoint object. This is permitted because ColoredPoint is a subclass of Point, so the class ColoredPoint is assignment compatible with the type Point. A ColoredPoint object includes support for all the methods of a Point. In addition to its particular fields r, g, and b, it has the fields of class Point, namely x and y.
- The local variable c has as its type the interface type Colorable, so it can hold a reference to any object whose class implements Colorable; specifically, it can hold a reference to a ColoredPoint.

Discussion: Note that an expression such as **new Colorable()** is not valid because it is not possible to create an instance of an interface, only of a class. Every array also has a class; the method **getClass**, when invoked for an array object, will return a class object (of class **Class**) that represents the class of the array.

The classes for arrays have strange names that are not valid identifiers; for example, the class for an array of **int** components has the name "[I" and so the value of the expression: new int[10].getClass().getName() is the string "[I"; see the specification of **Class.getName** for details.

3

Names

CONVENTIONS

Names are used to refer to entities declared in a program. A declared entity is a package, class type (normal or enum), interface type (normal or annotation type), member (class, interface, field, or method) of a reference type, type parametre (of a class, interface, method or constructor), parametre (to a method, constructor, or exception handler), or local variable. Names in programs are either simple, consisting of a single identifier, or qualified, consisting of a sequence of identifiers separated by "." tokens.

Every declaration that introduces a name has a *scope*, which is the part of the program text within which the declared entity can be referred to by a simple name. Packages and reference types (that is, class types, interface types, and array types) have members. A member can be referred to using a qualified name *N.x*, where *N* is a simple or qualified name and *x* is an identifier. If *N* names a package, then *x* is a member of that package, which is either a class or interface type or a subpackage. If *N* names a reference type or a variable of a reference type, then *x* names a member of that type, which is either a class, an interface, a field, or a method.

In determining the meaning of a name, the context of the occurrence is used to disambiguate among packages, types, variables, and methods with the same name. Access control can be specified in a class, interface, method, or field declaration to control when *access* to a member is allowed. Access is a different concept from scope; access specifies the part of the program text within which the declared entity can be referred to by a qualified name, a field access expression, or a method invocation expression in which the method is not specified by a simple name. The default access is that a member can be accessed anywhere within the package that contains its declaration; other possibilities are **`public`**, **`protected`**, and **`private`**.

Fully qualified and canonical names and naming conventions. The name of a field, parametre, or local variable may be used as an expression.The name of a method may appear in an expression only as part of a method invocation expression. The name of a class or interface type may appear in an expression only as part of a class literal, a qualified this expression, a class instance creation expression, an array creation expression, a cast expression, an **`instanceof`** expression, an enum constant, or as part of a qualified name for a field or method. The name of a package may appear in an expression only as part of a qualified name for a class or interface type.

DECLARATIONS

A *declaration* introduces an entity into a program and includes an identifier that can be used in a name to refer to this entity. A declared entity is one of the following:

- A package, declared in a package declaration
- An imported type, declared in a single-type-import declaration or a type-import-on-demand declaration
- A class, declared in a class type declaration
- An interface, declared in an interface type declaration
- A type variable, declared as a formal type parametre of a generic class, interface, method or constructor.
- A member of a reference type one of the following:
  - A member class.
  - A member interface.
  - an enum constant.
  - A field, one of the following:
- A field declared in a class type
- A constant field declared in an interface type

- The field length, which is implicitly a member of every array type
  - A method, one of the following:
- A method (abstract or otherwise) declared in a class type
- A method (always abstract) declared in an interface type
- A parametre, one of the following:
  - A parametre of a method or constructor of a class
  - A parametre of an abstract method of an interface
  - A parametre of an exception handler declared in a catch clause of a try statement
- A local variable, one of the following:
  - A local variable declared in a block
  - A local variable declared in a for statement

Constructors are also introduced by declarations, but use the name of the class in which they are declared rather than introducing a new name.

NAMES AND IDENTIFIERS

A *name* is used to refer to an entity declared in a program. There are two forms of names: simple names and qualified names. A *simple name* is a single identifier. A *qualified name* consists of a name, a " . " token, and an identifier.

In determining the meaning of a name, the context in which the name appears is taken into account. The rules of distinguish among contexts where a name must denote (refer to) a package, a type, a variable or value in an expression, or a method. Not all identifiers in programs are a part of a name. Identifiers are also used in the following situations:

- In declarations, where an identifier may occur to specify the name by which the declared entity will be known
- In field access expressions, where an identifier occurs after a "." token to indicate a member of an object that is the value of an expression or the keyword super that appears before the "." token
- In some method invocation expressions, where an

identifier may occur after a "." token and before a "(" token to indicate a method to be invoked for an object that is the value of an expression or the keyword super that appears before the "." token

- In qualified class instance creation expressions, where an identifier occurs immediately to the right of the leftmost new token to indicate a type that must be a member of the compile-time type of the primary expression preceding the "." preceding the leftmost new token.
- As labels in labeled statements and in break and continue statements that refer to statement labels.

In the example:

```
class Test {
    public static void main(String[] args) {
         Class c = System.out.getClass();
    System.out.println(c.toString().length() +
                   args[0].length() + args.length);
    }
}
```

the identifiers `Test`, `main`, and the first occurrences of `args` and `c` are not names; rather, they are used in declarations to specify the names of the declared entities.

The names **String, Class, System.out.getClass, System.out.println, c.toString, args,** and **args.length** appear in the example. The first occurrence of **length** is not a name, but rather an identifier appearing in a method invocation expression.

The second occurrence of `length` is not a name, but rather an identifier appearing in a method invocation expression. The identifiers used in labeled statements and their associated `break` and `continue` statements are completely separate from those used in declarations.

Thus, the following code is valid:

```
class TestString {
    char[] value;
    int offset, count;
    int indexOf(TestString str, int fromIndex)
```

```
    {
    char[] v1 = value, v2 = str.value;
    int max = offset + (count - str.count);
    int start = offset + ((fromIndex < 0) ? 0 :
    fromIndex);
    i:
    for (int i = start; i <= max; i++)
    {
    int n = str.count, j = i, k = str.offset;
    while (n– != 0) {
    if (v1[j++] != v2[k++])
                        continue i;
                }
                return i - offset;
        }
        return -1;
    }
}
```

This code was taken from a version of the class String and its method indexOf, where the label was originally called test. Changing the label to have the same name as the local variable i does not obscure the label in the scope of the declaration of i.

The identifier max could also have been used as the statement label; the label would not obscure the local variable max within the labeled statement.

SCOPE OF A DECLARATION

The *scope* of a declaration is the region of the program within which the entity declared by the declaration can be referred to using a simple name (provided it is visible). A declaration is said to be *in scope* at a particular point in a program if and only if the declaration's scope includes that point.

The scoping rules for various constructs are given in the sections that describe those constructs. For convenience, the rules are repeated here: The scope of the declaration of an observable top level package is all observable compilation units. The declaration of a package that is not observable is never in scope. Subpackage declarations are never in scope. The scope of a type imported by a single-type-import declaration or a type-import-on-demand declaration is all the class and interface type declarations in the compilation unit in which the import declaration appears.

The scope of a member imported by a single-static-import declaration or a static-import-on-demand declaration is all the class and interface type declarations in the compilation unit in which the import declaration appears. The scope of a top level type is all type declarations in the package in which the top level type is declared.

The scope of a declaration of a member *m* declared in or inherited by a class type *C* is the entire body of *C*, including any nested type declarations. The scope of the declaration of a member *m* declared in or inherited by an interface type *I* is the entire body of *I*, including any nested type declarations. The scope of a parametre of a method or constructor is the entire body of the method or constructor.

The scope of an interface's type parametre is the entire declaration of the interface including the type parametre section itself. Therefore, type parametres can appear as parts of their own bounds, or as bounds of other type parametres declared in the same section.

The scope of a method's type parametre is the entire declaration of the method, including the type parametre section itself. Therefore, type parametres can appear as parts of their own bounds, or as bounds of other type parametres declared in the same section.

The scope of a constructor's type parametre is the entire declaration of the constructor, including the type parametre section itself. Therefore, type parametres can appear as parts of their own bounds, or as bounds of other type parametres declared in the same section. The scope of a local variable declaration in a block is the rest of the block in which the declaration appears, starting with its own initializer and including any further declarators to the right in the local variable declaration statement. The scope of a local class immediately enclosed by a block is the rest of the immediately enclosing block, including its own class declaration. The scope of a local class immediately enclosed by in a switch block statement group is the rest of the immediately enclosing switch block statement group, including its own class declaration.

The scope of a local variable declared in the *forInit* part of a basic `for` statement includes all of the following:

- Its own initializer
- Any further declarators to the right in the *ForInit* part of the for statement
- The *Expression* and *ForUpdate* parts of the for statement
- The contained *Statement*

The scope of a local variable declared in the *FormalParametre* part of an enhanced `for` statement is the contained *Statement* The scope of a parametre of an exception handler that is declared in a `catch` clause of a `try` statement is the entire block associated with the `catch`. These rules imply that declarations of class and interface types need not appear before uses of the types.

In the example:

```
package points;
class Point {
        int x, y;
        PointList list;
        Point next;
}
class PointList {
        Point first;
}
```

the use of `PointList` in class `Point` is correct, because the scope of the class declaration `PointList` includes both class `Point` and class `PointList`, as well as any other type declarations in other compilation units of package `points`.

SHADOWING DECLARATIONS

Some declarations may be *shadowed* in part of their scope by another declaration of the same name, in which case a simple name cannot be used to refer to the declared entity. A declaration *d* of a type named *n* shadows the declarations of any other types named *n* that are in scope at the point where *d* occurs throughout the scope of *d*. A declaration *d* of a field, local variable, method parametre, constructor parametre or exception handler parametre named *n* shadows the declarations of any other fields, local variables, method parametres, constructor parametres or exception handler parametres named *n* that are in scope at the point where *d* occurs throughout the scope of *d*.

A declaration *d* of a method named *n* shadows the declarations of any other methods named *n* that are in an enclosing scope at the point where *d* occurs throughout the scope of *d*. A package declaration never shadows any other declaration.

A single-type-import declaration *d* in a compilation unit *c* of package *p* that imports a type named *n* shadows the declarations of:

- Any top level type named *n* declared in another compilation unit of *p*.
- Any type named *n* imported by a type-import-on-demand declaration in *c*.
- Any type named *n* imported by a static-import-on-demand declaration in *c*.

A single-static-import declaration *d* in a compilation unit *c* of package *p* that imports a field named *n* shadows the declaration of any static field named *n* imported by a static-import-on-demand declaration in *c*, throughout *c*. A single-static-import declaration *d* in a compilation unit *c* of package *p* that imports a method named *n* with signature s shadows the declaration of any static method named *n* with signature *s* imported by a static-import-on-demand declaration in *c*, throughout *c*. A single-static-import declaration *d* in a compilation unit *c* of package *p* that imports a type named *n* shadows the declarations of:

- Any static type named *n* imported by a static-import-on-demand declaration in *c*.
- Any top level type named *n* declared in another compilation unit of *p*.

- Any type named *n* imported by a type-import-on-demand declaration in *c*.

```
throughout c.
```

A type-import-on-demand declaration never causes any other declaration to be shadowed. A static-import-on-demand declaration never causes any other declaration to be shadowed. A declaration *d* is said to be *visible at point p in a program* if the scope of *d* includes *p*, and *d* is not shadowed by any other declaration at *p*. When the program point we are discussing is clear from context, we will often simply say that a declaration is *visible*. Note that shadowing is distinct from hiding. Hiding, in the technical sense defined in this specification, applies only to members which would otherwise be inherited but are not because of a declaration in a subclass. Shadowing is also distinct from obscuring.

Here is an example of shadowing of a field declaration by a local variable declaration:

```
class Test {
    static int x = 1;
    public static void main(String[] args) {
         int x = 0;
         System.out.print("x=" + x);
         System.out.println(", Test.x=" +
    Test.x);
    }
}
produces the output:
x=0, Test.x=1
```

This example declares:

- A class Test
- A class (static) variable x that is a member of the class Test
- A class method main that is a member of the class Test
- A parametre args of the main method.
- A local variable x of the main method

Since the scope of a class variable includes the entire body of the class the class variable **x** would normally be available throughout the entire body of the method **`main`**. In this example, however, the class variable **`x`** is shadowed within the body of the method **`main`** by the declaration of the local variable **`x`**. A local variable has as its scope the rest of the block in which it is declared; in this case this is the rest of the body of the **`main`** method, namely its initializer "`0`" and the invocations of **`print`** and **`println`**.

This means that:

- The expression "x" in the invocation of print refers to (denotes) the value of the local variable x.
- The invocation of println uses a qualified name Test.x, which uses the class type name Test to access the class variable x, because the declaration of Test.x is shadowed at this point and cannot be referred to by its simple name.

The following example illustrates the shadowing of one type declaration by another:

```
import java.util.*;
class Vector {
    int val[] = { 1 , 2 };
}
class Test {
    public static void main(String[] args) {
        Vector v = new Vector();
        System.out.println(v.val[0]);
    }
}
compiles and prints:
1
```

using the class **`Vector`** declared here in preference to the generic class **`java.util.Vector`** that might be imported on demand.

OBSCURED DECLARATIONS

A simple name may occur in contexts where it may potentially be interpreted as the name of a variable, a type or a package. In these situations, the rules of specify that a variable will be chosen in preference to a type, and that a type will be chosen in preference to a package. Thus, it is may sometimes be impossible to refer to a visible type or package declaration via its simple name. We say that such a declaration is *obscured*.

MEMBERS OF A PACKAGE

The members of a package are specified in. For convenience, we repeat that specification here: The members of a package are its subpackages and all the top level class types and top level interface types declared in all the compilation units of the package. In general, the subpackages of a package are determined by the host system. However, the package `java` always includes the subpackages `lang` and `io` and may include other subpackages. No two distinct members of the same package may have the same simple name, but members of different packages may have the same simple name.

For example, it is possible to declare a package:

```
package vector;
public class Vector { Object[] vec; }
```

that has as a member a `public` class named `Vector`, even though the package `java.util` also declares a class named `Vector`. These two class types are different, reflected by the fact that they have different fully qualified names.The fully qualified name of this example `Vector` is `vector.Vector`, whereas `java.util.Vector` is the fully qualified name of the `Vector` class usually included in the Java platform. Because the package `vector` contains a class named `Vector`, it cannot also have a subpackage named `Vector`.

THE MEMBERS OF A CLASS TYPE

The members of a class type are classes, interfaces, fields, and methods. Members are either declared in the type, or *inherited* because they are accessible members of a superclass or superinterface which are neither private nor hidden nor overridden.

The members of a class type are all of the following:

- Members inherited from its direct superclass, if it has one (the class Object has no direct superclass)

- Members inherited from any direct superinterfaces
- Members declared in the body of the class

Constructors and type variables are not members.

There is no restriction against a field and a method of a class type having the same simple name. Likewise, there is no restriction against a member class or member interface of a class type having the same simple name as a field or method of that class type.

A class may have two or more fields with the same simple name if they are declared in different interfaces and inherited. An attempt to refer to any of the fields by its simple name results in a compile-time error.

```
In the example:
interface Colors {
    int WHITE = 0, BLACK = 1;
}
interface Separates {
    int CYAN = 0, MAGENTA = 1, YELLOW = 2,
    BLACK = 3;
}
class Test implements Colors, Separates {
    public static void main(String[] args) {
         System.out.println(BLACK); // compile-
    time error: ambiguous
    }
}
```

the name **BLACK** in the method **main** is ambiguous, because class **Test** has two members named **BLACK**, one inherited from **Colors** and one from **Separates**.

A class type may have two or more methods with the same simple name if the methods have signatures that are not override-equivalent.Such a method member name is said to be *overloaded*. A class type may contain a declaration for a method with the same name and the same signature as a method that would otherwise be inherited from a superclass or superinterface. In this case, the method of the superclass or superinterface is not inherited. If the method not inherited is **abstract**, then the new declaration is said to *implement* it; if the method not inherited is not **abstract**, then the new declaration is said to *override* it.

In the example:

```
class Point {
    float x, y;
    void move(int dx, int dy) { x += dx; y +=
    dy; }
    void move(float dx, float dy) { x += dx; y
    += dy; }
    public String toString() { return
    "("+x+","+y+")"; }
}
```

the class **Point** has two members that are methods with the same name, **move**. The overloaded **move** method of class **Point** chosen for any particular method invocation is determined at compile time by the overloading resolution procedure given in.

In this example, the members of the class **Point** are the **float** instance variables **x** and **y** declared in **Point**, the two declared **move** methods, the declared **toString** method, and the members that **Point** inherits from its implicit direct superclass **Object**, such as the method **hashCode**. Note that **Point** does not inherit the **toString** method of class **Object** because that method is overridden by the declaration of the **toString** method in class **Point**.

THE MEMBERS OF AN INTERFACE TYPE

The members of an interface type may be classes, interfaces, fields, and methods.

The members of an interface are:

- Those members declared in the interface.
- Those members inherited from direct superinterfaces.
- If an interface has no direct superinterfaces, then the interface implicitly declares a public abstract member method *m* with signature *s*, return type *r*, and throws clause *t* corresponding to each public instance method *m* with signature *s*, return type *r*, and throws clause *t* declared in Object, unless a method with the

same signature, same return type, and a compatible throws clause is explicitly declared by the interface. It is a compile-time error if the interface explicitly declares such a method *m* in the case where *m* is declared to be final in Object.

Type variables are not members: An interface may have two or more fields with the same simple name if they are declared in different interfaces and inherited. An attempt to refer to any such field by its simple name results in a compile-time error.

In the example:

```
interface Colors {
    int WHITE = 0, BLACK = 1;
}
interface Separates {
    int CYAN = 0, MAGENTA = 1, YELLOW = 2,
    BLACK = 3;
}
interface ColorsAndSeparates extends Colors,
    Separates {
         int DEFAULT = BLACK;// compile-time
    error: ambiguous
}
```

the members of the interface `ColorsAndSeparates` include those members inherited from `Colors` and those inherited from `Separates`, namely `WHITE`, `BLACK` (first of two), `CYAN`, `MAGENTA`, `YELLOW`, and `BLACK` (second of two). The member name `BLACK` is ambiguous in the interface `ColorsAnd Separates`.

THE MEMBERS OF AN ARRAY TYPE

The members of an array type are specified in. For convenience, we repeat that specification here.

The members of an array type are all of the following:

- The public final field length, which contains the number of components of the array (length may be positive or zero).
- The public method clone, which overrides the method of the same name in class Object and throws

no checked exceptions. The return type of the clone method of an array type *T[]* is *T[]*.

- All the members inherited from class Object; the only method of Object that is not inherited is its clone method.

The example:

```
class Test {
    public static void main(String[] args) {
        int[] ia = new int[3];
        int[] ib = new int[6];
        System.out.println(ia.getClass() ==
    ib.getClass());
        System.out.println("ia has length="
    + ia.length);
    }
}
produces the output:
true
ia has length=3
```

This example uses the method `getClass` inherited from class `Object` and the field `length`. The result of the comparison of the `Class` objects in the first `println` demonstrates that all arrays whose components are of type `int` are instances of the same array type, which is `int[]`.

DETERMINING THE MEANING OF A NAME

The meaning of a name depends on the context in which it is used. The determination of the meaning of a name requires three steps

First, context causes a name syntactically to fall into one of six categories: *PackageName, TypeName, ExpressionName, MethodName, PackageOrTypeName,* or *AmbiguousName.*

Second, a name that is initially classified by its context as an *AmbiguousName* or as a *PackageOrTypeName* is then reclassified to be a *PackageName, TypeName,* or *ExpressionName.* Third, the resulting category then dictates the final determination of the meaning of the name (or a compilation error if the name has no meaning).

```
PackageName:
    Identifier
    PackageName. Identifier
TypeName:
    Identifier
    PackageOrTypeName. Identifier
ExpressionName:
    Identifier
    AmbiguousName. Identifier
MethodName:
    Identifier
    AmbiguousName. Identifier
PackageOrTypeName:
    Identifier
    PackageOrTypeName. Identifier
AmbiguousName:
    Identifier
    AmbiguousName. Identifier
```

The use of context helps to minimize name conflicts between entities of different kinds. Such conflicts will be rare if the naming conventions described in are followed. Nevertheless, conflicts may arise unintentionally as types developed by different programmers or different organizations evolve. For example, types, methods, and fields may have the same name. It is always possible to distinguish between a method and a field with the same name, since the context of a use always tells whether a method is intended.

SYNTACTIC CLASSIFICATION OF A NAME ACCORDING TO CONTEXT

A name is syntactically classified as a PackageName in these contexts:

- In a package declaration
- To the left of the "." in a qualified *PackageName*

A name is syntactically classified as a TypeName in these contexts:

- In a single-type-import declaration
- To the left of the "." in a single static import declaration

- To the left of the "." in a static import-on-demand declaration
- To the left of the "<" in a parametreized type
- In an actual type argument list of a parametreized type
- In an explicit actual type argument list in a generic method or constructor invocation
- In an extends clause in a type variable declaration
- In an extends clause of a wildcard type argument
- In a super clause of a wildcard type argument
- In an extends clause in a class declaration
- In an implements clause in a class declaration
- In an extends clause in an interface declaration
- After the "@" sign in an annotation
- As a *Type* (or the part of a *Type* that remains after all brackets are deleted) in any of the following contexts:
  - In a field declaration
  - As the result type of a method
  - As the type of a formal parametre of a method or constructor
  - As the type of an exception that can be thrown by a method or constructor
  - As the type of a local variable
  - As the type of an exception parametre in a catch clause of a try statement
  - As the type in a class literal
  - As the qualifying type of a qualified this expression.
  - As the class type which is to be instantiated in an unqualified class instance creation expression
  - As the direct superclass or direct superinterface of an anonymous class which is to be instantiated in an unqualified class instance creation expression
  - As the element type of an array to be created in an array creation expression
  - As the qualifying type of field access using the keyword super

   — As the qualifying type of a method invocation using the keyword super
   — As the type mentioned in the cast operator of a cast expression
   — As the type that follows the instanceof relational operator

A name is syntactically classified as an ExpressionName in these contexts:

- As the qualifying expression in a qualified superclass constructor invocation
- As the qualifying expression in a qualified class instance creation expression
- As the array reference expression in an array access expression
- As a *PostfixExpression*
- As the left-hand operand of an assignment operator

A name is syntactically classified as a MethodName in these contexts:

- Before the "(" in a method invocation expression
- To the left of the "=" sign in an annotation's element value pair

A name is syntactically classified as a PackageOrTypeName in these contexts:

- To the left of the "." in a qualified TypeName
- In a type-import-on-demand declaration

A name is syntactically classified as an AmbiguousName in these contexts:

- To the left of the "." in a qualified *ExpressionName*
- To the left of the "." in a qualified *MethodName*
- To the left of the "." in a qualified *AmbiguousName*
- In the default value clause of an annotation type element declaration
- To the right of an "=" in an an element value pair

RECLASSIFICATION OF CONTEXTUALLY AMBIGUOUS NAMES

An *AmbiguousName* is then reclassified as follows:

- If the *AmbiguousName* is a simple name, consisting of a single *Identifier*:

- If the *Identifier* appears within the scope of a local variable declaration or parametre declaration or field declaration with that name, then the *AmbiguousName* is reclassified as an *ExpressionName.*
- Otherwise, if a field of that name is declared in the compilation unit containing the *Identifier* by a single-static-import declaration, or by a static-import-on-demand declaration then the *AmbiguousName* is reclassified as an *Expression Name.*
- Otherwise, if the *Identifier* appears within the scope of a top level class or interface type declaration, a local class declaration or member type declaration with that name, then the *AmbiguousName* is reclassified as a *TypeName.*
- Otherwise, if a type of that name is declared in the compilation unit containing the *Identifier,* either by a single-type-import declaration, or by a type-import-on-demand declaration, or by a single-static-import declaration, or by a static-import-on-demand declaration, then the *AmbiguousName* is reclassified as a *TypeName.*
- Otherwise, the *AmbiguousName* is reclassified as a *PackageName.* A later step determines whether or not a package of that name actually exists.

• If the *AmbiguousName* is a qualified name, consisting of a name, a ".", and an *Identifier,* then the name to the left of the "." is first reclassified, for it is itself an *AmbiguousName.* There is then a choice:

- If the name to the left of the "." is reclassified as a *PackageName,* then if there is a package whose name is the name to the left of the "." and that package contains a declaration of a type whose name is the same as the *Identifier,* then this *AmbiguousName* is reclassified as a *TypeName.* Otherwise, this *AmbiguousName* is reclassified as a *PackageName.* A later step determines whether or not a package of that name actually exists.

— If the name to the left of the "." is reclassified as a *TypeName*, then if the *Identifier* is the name of a method or field of the type denoted by TypeName, this *AmbiguousName* is reclassified as an *ExpressionName.* Otherwise, if the Identifier is the name of a member type of the type denoted by TypeName, this AmbiguousName is reclassified as a TypeName. Otherwise, a compile-time error results.

— If the name to the left of the "." is reclassified as an *ExpressionName,* then let T be the type of the expression denoted by ExpressionName. If the Identifier is the name of a method or field of the type denoted by T, this *AmbiguousName* is reclassified as an *ExpressionName.* Otherwise, if the Identifier is the name of a member type of the type denoted by T, then this Ambiguous Name is reclassified as a TypeName. Otherwise, a compile-time error results.

As an example, consider the following contrived "library code":

```
package org.rpgpoet;
import java.util.Random;
interface Music { Random[] wizards = new
Random[4]; }
```

and then consider this example code in another package:

```
package bazola;
class Gabriel {
static int n = org. rpgpoet. Music. wizards.
length;
}
```

First of all, the name org.rpgpoet.Music.wizards.length is classified as an *ExpressionName* because it functions as a *PostfixExpression*. Therefore, each of the names:

```
org.rpgpoet.Music.wizards
org.rpgpoet.Music
org.rpgpoet
org
```

is initially classified as an *AmbiguousName.* These are then reclassified:

- The simple name org is reclassified as a *PackageName* (since there is no variable or type named org in scope).
- Next, assuming that there is no class or interface named rpgpoet in any compilation unit of package org (and we know that there is no such class or interface because package org has a subpackage named rpgpoet), the qualified name org.rpgpoet is reclassified as a *PackageName.*
- Next, because package org.rpgpoet has an interface type named Music, the qualified name org.rpgpoet. Music is reclassified as a *TypeName.*
- Finally, because the name org.rpgpoet.Music is a *TypeName,* the qualified name org.rpgpoet.Music. wizards is reclassified as an *ExpressionName.*

MEANING OF PACKAGE NAMES

The meaning of a name classified as a *PackageName* is determined as follows.

Simple Package Names

If a package name consists of a single *Identifier,* then this identifier denotes a top level package named by that identifier. If no top level package of that name is in scope, then a compile-time error occurs.

QUALIFIED PACKAGE NAMES

If a package name is of the form *Q*.*Id,* then *Q* must also be a package name. The package name *Q*.*Id* names a package that is the member named *Id* within the package named by *Q.* If *Q* does not name an observable package, or *Id* is not the simple name an observable subpackage of that package, then a compile-time error occurs.

PACKAGE OR TYPENAMES

SIMPLE PACKAGEORTYPENAMES

If the *PackageOrTypeName, Q,* occurs in the scope of a type named KQ, then the *PackageOrTypeName* is reclassified as a *TypeName*. Otherwise, the *PackageOrTypeName* is reclassified as a *PackageName*. The meaning of the *PackageOrTypeName* is the meaning of the reclassified name.

QUALIFIED PACKAGE OR TYPENAMES

Given a qualified *PackageOrTypeName* of the form *Q.Id*, if the type or package denoted by *Q* has a member type named *Id*, then the qualified *PackageOrTypeName* name is reclassified as a *TypeName*.

Otherwise, it is reclassified as a *PackageName*. The meaning of the qualified *PackageOrTypeName* is the meaning of the reclassified name.

MEANING OF TYPE NAMES

The meaning of a name classified as a *TypeName* is determined as follows.

SIMPLE TYPE NAMES

If a type name consists of a single *Identifier*, then the identifier must occur in the scope of exactly one visible declaration of a type with this name, or a compile-time error occurs. The meaning of the type name is that type.

QUALIFIED TYPE NAMES

If a type name is of the form *Q*.*Id*, then *Q* must be either a type name or a package name. If *Id* names exactly one type that is a member of the type or package denoted by *Q*, then the qualified type name denotes that type.

If *Id* does not name a member type within *Q*, or the member type named *Id* within *Q* is not accessible, or *Id* names more than one member type within *Q*, then a compile-time error occurs.

```
The example:
package wnj.test;
class Test {
    public static void main(String[] args) {
         java.util.Date date =
```

```
        new java.util.Date(System.current
    TimeMillis());

    System.out.println(date.toLocaleString());
    }
}
```

produced the following output the first time it was run:

```
Sun Jan 21 22:56:29 1996
```

In this example the name `java.util.Date` must denote a type, so we first use the procedure recursively to determine if `java.util` is an accessible type or a package, which it is, and then look to see if the type `Date` is accessible in this package. Discussion: Type names are distinct from type declaration specifiers.A type name is always qualified by meas of another type name. In some cases, it is necessary to access an inner class that is a member of a parametreized type:

```
class GenericOuter<T extends Number> {
    public class Inner<S extends Comparable<S>>
    {
        T getT() { return null;}
        S getS() { return null;}
    }
};
GenericOuter<Integer>.Inner<Double> x1 = null;
Integer i = x1.getT();
Double d = x1.getS();
If we accessed Inner by qualifying it with a
    type name, as in:
GenericOuter.Inner x2 = null;
```

we would force its use as a raw type, losing type information.

MEANING OF EXPRESSION NAMES

The meaning of a name classified as an *ExpressionName* is determined as follows.

SIMPLE EXPRESSION NAMES

If an expression name consists of a single *Identifier*, then there must be exactly one visible declaration denoting either a local variable, parametre or field in scope at the point at which the the *Identifier* occurs. Otherwise, a compile-time error occurs. If the declaration declares a final field, the meaning of the name is the value of that field. Otherwise, the meaning of the expression name is the variable declared by the declaration.

If the field is an instance variable, the expression name must appear within the declaration of an instance method, constructor, instance initializer, or instance variable initializer. If it appears within a `static` method, static initializer,or initializer for a `static` variable, then a compile-time error occurs. The type of the expression name is the declared type of the field, local variable or parametre after capture conversion.

In the example:

```
class Test {
    static int v;
    static final int f = 3;
    public static void main(String[] args) {
        int i;
        i = 1;
        v = 2;
        f = 33; // compile-time error
    System.out.println(i + " " + v + " " + f);
    }
}
```

the names used as the left-hand-sides in the assignments to `i`, `v`, and `f` denote the local variable `i`, the field `v`, and the value of `f` (not the variable `f`, because `f` is a `final` variable). The example therefore produces an error at compile time because the last assignment does not have a variable as its left-hand side. If the erroneous assignment is removed, the modified code can be compiled and it will produce the output:

```
1 2 3
```

QUALIFIED EXPRESSION NAMES

If an expression name is of the form *Q*.*Id*, then *Q* has already been classified as a package name, a type name, or an expression name:

- If *Q* is a package name, then a compile-time error occurs.
- If *Q* is a type name that names a class type, then:
  - If there is not exactly one accessible member of the class type that is a field named *Id*, then a compile-time error occurs.
  - Otherwise, if the single accessible member field is not a class variable (that is, it is not declared static), then a compile-time error occurs.
  - Otherwise, if the class variable is declared final, then *Q.Id* denotes the value of the class variable. The type of the expression *Q.Id* is the declared type of the class variable after capture conversion. If *Q.Id* appears in a context that requires a variable and not a value, then a compile-time error occurs.
  - Otherwise, *Q.Id* denotes the class variable. The type of the expression *Q.Id* is the declared type of the class variable after capture conversion. Note that this clause covers the use of enum constants, since these always have a corresponding final class variable.
- If *Q* is a type name that names an interface type, then:
  - If there is not exactly one accessible member of the interface type that is a field named *Id*, then a compile-time error occurs.
  - Otherwise, *Q.Id* denotes the value of the field. The type of the expression *Q.Id* is the declared type of the field after capture conversion. If *Q.Id* appears in a context that requires a variable and not a value, then a compile-time error occurs.
- If *Q* is an expression name, let *T* be the type of the expression *Q*:
  - If *T* is not a reference type, a compile-time error occurs.
  - If there is not exactly one accessible member of the type *T* that is a field named *Id*, then a compile-time error occurs.
  - Otherwise, if this field is any of the following:

- A field of an interface type
- A final field of a class type (which may be either a class variable or an instance variable)
- The final field length of an array type then *Q.Id* denotes the value of the field. The type of the expression *Q.Id* is the declared type of the field after capture conversion. If *Q.Id* appears in a context that requires a variable and not a value, then a compile-time error occurs.
  - Otherwise, *Q.Id* denotes a variable, the field *Id* of class *T*, which may be either a class variable or an instance variable. The type of the expression *Q.Id* is the type of the field member after capture conversion.

The example:

```
class Point {
        int x, y;
        static int nPoints;
}
class Test {
    public static void main(String[] args) {
        int i = 0;
        i.x++; // compile-time error
        Point p = new Point();
        p.nPoints(); // compile-time error
    }
}
```

encounters two compile-time errors, because the `int` variable `i` has no members, and because `nPoints` is not a method of class `Point`.

Discussion: Note that expression names may be qualified by type names, but not by types in general. A consequence is that it is not possible to access a class variable through a parametreized type

```
class Foo<T> {
    public static int classVar = 42;
}
Foo<String>.classVar = 91; // illegal
```

```
Instead, one writes
Foo.classVar = 91;
```

This does not restrict the language in any meaningful way. Type parametres may not be used in the types of static variables, and so the actual parametres of a parametreized type can never influence the type of a static variable. Therefore, no expressive power is lost. Technically, the type name `Foo` above is a raw type, but this use of raw types is harmless, and does not give rise to warnings.

MEANING OF METHOD NAMES

A *MethodName* can appear only in a method invocation expression or as an element name in an element-value pair. The meaning of a name classified as a *MethodName* is determined as follows.

SIMPLE METHOD NAMES

A simple method name may appear as the element name in an element-value pair. The *Identifier* in an *ElementValuePair* must be the simple name of one of the elements of the annotation type identified by *TypeName* in the containing annotation. Otherwise, a compile-time error occurs. (In other words, the identifier in an element-value pair must also be a method name in the interface identified by *TypeName*.)

Otherwise, a simple method name necessarily appears in the context of a method invocation expression. In that case, if a method name consists of a single *Identifier*, then *Identifier* is the method name to be used for method invocation. The *Identifier* must name at least one visible method that is in scope at the point where the *Identifier* appear or a method imported by a single-static-import declaration or static-import-on-demand declaration within the compilation unit within which the *Identifier* appears.

QUALIFIED METHOD NAMES

A qualified method name can only appear in the context of a method invocation expression. If a method name is of the form *Q.Id*, then *Q* has already been classified as a package name, a type name, or an expression name. If *Q* is a package name, then a compile-time error occurs. Otherwise, *Id* is the method name to be used for method invocation. If *Q* is a type name, then *Id* must name at least one **`static`** method of the type *Q*. If *Q* is an expression name, then let *T* be the type of the expression *Q*; *Id* must name at least one method of the type *T*.

ACCESS CONTROL

The Java programming language provides mechanisms for *access control*, to prevent the users of a package or class from depending on unnecessary details of the implementation of that package or class. If access is permitted, then the accessed entity is said to be *accessible*.

Note that accessibility is a static property that can be determined at compile time; it depends only on types and declaration modifiers. Qualified names are a means of access to members of packages and reference types; related means of access include field access expressions and method invocation expressions. All three are syntactically similar in that a "`.`" token appears, preceded by some indication of a package, type, or expression having a type and followed by an *Identifier* that names a member of the package or type. These are collectively known as constructs for *qualified access*. Access control applies to qualified access and to the invocation of constructors by class instance creation expressions and explicit constructor invocations. Accessibility also effects inheritance of class members, including hiding and method overriding.

DETERMINING ACCESSIBILITY

- A package is always accessible.
- If a class or interface type is declared public, then it may be accessed by any code, provided that the compilation unit in which it is declared is observable. If a top level class or interface type is not declared public, then it may be accessed only from within the package in which it is declared.
- An array type is accessible if and only if its element type is accessible.
- A member (class, interface, field, or method) of a

reference type or a constructor of a class type is accessible only if the type is accessible and the member or constructor is declared to permit access:

— If the member or constructor is declared public, then access is permitted. All members of interfaces are implicitly public.

— Otherwise, if the member or constructor is declared protected, then access is permitted only when one of the following is true:

- Access to the member or constructor occurs from within the package containing the class in which the protected member or constructor is declared.
- Access is correct as described in.

— Otherwise, if the member or constructor is declared private, then access is permitted if and only if it occurs within the body of the top level class that encloses the declaration of the member or constructor.

— Otherwise, we say there is default access, which is permitted only when the access occurs from within the package in which the type is declared.

DETAILS ON PROTECTED ACCESS

A `protected` member or constructor of an object may be accessed from outside the package in which it is declared only by code that is responsible for the implementation of that object.

ACCESS TO A PROTECTED MEMBER

Let C be the class in which a `protected` member `m` is declared. Access is permitted only within the body of a subclass *S* of C. In addition, if *Id* denotes an instance field or instance method, then:

- If the access is by a qualified name *Q.Id*, where *Q* is an *ExpressionName*, then the access is permitted if and only if the type of the expression *Q* is *S* or a subclass of *S*.
- If the access is by a field access expression *E.Id*, where *E* is a *Primary* expression, or by a method invocation expression *E.Id*(...), where *E* is a *Primary* expression,

then the access is permitted if and only if the type of *E* is *S* or a subclass of *S*.

QUALIFIED ACCESS TO A PROTECTED CONSTRUCTOR

Let *C* be the class in which a **`protected`** constructor is declared and let *S* be the innermost class in whose declaration the use of the **`protected`** constructor occurs. Then:

- If the access is by a superclass constructor invocation super(...) or by a qualified superclass constructor invocation of the form *E*.super(...), where *E* is a *Primary* expression, then the access is permitted.
- If the access is by an anonymous class instance creation expression of the form new *C*(...){...} or by a qualified class instance creation expression of the form *E*.new *C*(...){...}, where *E* is a *Primary* expression, then the access is permitted.
- Otherwise, if the access is by a simple class instance creation expression of the form new *C*(...) or by a qualified class instance creation expression of the form *E*.new *C*(...), where *E* is a *Primary* expression, then the access is not permitted. A protected constructor can be accessed by a class instance creation expression (that does not declare an anonymous class) only from within the package in which it is defined.

AN EXAMPLE OF ACCESS CONTROL

For examples of access control, consider the two compilation units:

```
package points;
class PointVec { Point[] vec; }
```

and:

```
package points;
public class Point {
    protected int x, y;
    public void move(int dx, int dy) { x += dx;
    y += dy; }
```

```
    public int getX() { return x; }
    public int getY() { return y; }
}
```

which declare two class types in the package points:

- The class type PointVec is not public and not part of the public interface of the package points, but rather can be used only by other classes in the package.
- The class type Point is declared public and is available to other packages. It is part of the public interface of the package points.
- The methods move, getX, and getY of the class Point are declared public and so are available to any code that uses an object of type Point.
- The fields x and y are declared protected and are accessible outside the package points only in subclasses of class Point, and only when they are fields of objects that are being implemented by the code that is accessing them.

EXAMPLE: ACCESS TO PUBLIC AND NON-PUBLIC CLASSES

If a class lacks the `public` modifier, access to the class declaration is limited to the package in which it is declared. In the example:

```
package points;
public class Point {
    public int x, y;
    public void move(int dx, int dy) { x += dx;
    y += dy; }
}
class PointList {
    Point next, prev;
}
```

two classes are declared in the compilation unit. The class `Point` is available outside the package `points`, while the class `PointList` is available for access only within the package.

Thus a compilation unit in another package can access `points.Point`, either by using its fully qualified name:

```
package pointsUser;
class Test {
    public static void main(String[] args) {
        points.Point p = new points.Point();
        System.out.println(p.x + " " + p.y);
    }
}
```

or by using a single-type-import declaration that mentions the fully qualified name, so that the simple name may be used thereafter:

```
package pointsUser;
import points.Point;
class Test {
    public static void main(String[] args) {
        Point p = new Point();
        System.out.println(p.x + " " + p.y);
    }}
```

However, this compilation unit cannot use or import `points.PointList`, which is not declared `public` and is therefore inaccessible outside package `points`.

DEFAULT-ACCESS FIELDS, METHODS, AND CONSTRUCTORS

If none of the access modifiers `public`, `protected`, or `private` are specified, a class member or constructor is accessible throughout the package that contains the declaration of the class in which the class member is declared, but the class member or constructor is not accessible in any other package.

If a `public` class has a method or constructor with default access, then this method or constructor is not accessible to or inherited by a subclass declared outside this package.

```
For example, if we have:
package points;
public class Point {
    public int x, y;
    void move(int dx, int dy) { x += dx; y +=
    dy; }
    public void moveAlso(int dx, int dy) {
```

```
    move(dx, dy); }
}
```

then a subclass in another package may declare an unrelated `move` method, with the same signature and return type. Because the original `move` method is not accessible from package `morepoints`, `super` may not be used:

```
package morepoints;
public class PlusPoint extends points.Point {
    public void move(int dx, int dy) {
    super.move(dx,                          dy);
    // compile-time error
    moveAlso(dx, dy);
    }
}
```

Because move of `Point` is not overridden by `move` in `PlusPoint`, the method `moveAlso` in `Point` never calls the method move in `PlusPoint`. Thus if you delete the `super.move` call from `PlusPoint` and execute the test program:

```
   import points.Point;
import morepoints.PlusPoint;
class Test {
    public static void main(String[] args) {
         PlusPoint pp = new PlusPoint();
         pp.move(1, 1);
    }
}
```

it terminates normally. If move of `Point` were overridden by `move` in `PlusPoint`, then this program would recurse infinitely, until a `StackoverflowError` occurred.

PUBLIC FIELDS, METHODS, AND CONSTRUCTORS

A `public` class member or constructor is accessible throughout the package where it is declared and from any other package, provided the package in which it is declared is observable.

For example, in the compilation unit:

```
package points;
```

```
public class Point {
    int x, y;
    public void move(int dx, int dy) {
        x += dx; y += dy;
        moves++;
    }
    public static int moves = 0;
}
```

the `public` class `Point` has as `public` members the `move` method and the `moves` field. These `public` members are accessible to any other package that has access to package `points`. The fields `x` and `y` are not `public` and therefore are accessible only from within the package `points`.

PROTECTED FIELDS, METHODS, AND CONSTRUCTORS

Consider this example, where the `points` package declares:

```
   package points;
public class Point {
    protected int x, y;
    void warp(threePoint.Point3d a) {
    if (a.z > 0) // compile-time error: cannot
    access a.z
        a.delta(this);
    }
}
and the threePoint package declares:
package threePoint;
import points.Point;
public class Point3d extends Point {
    protected int z;
    public void delta(Point p) {
    p.x += this.x; // compile-time error: cannot
    access p.x
    p.y += this.y; // compile-time error: cannot
    access p.y
    }
```

```
    public void delta3d(Point3d q) {
        q.x += this.x;
        q.y += this.y;
        q.z += this.z;
    }
}
```

which defines a class **Point3d**. A compile-time error occurs in the method **delta** here: it cannot access the protected members **x** and **y** of its parametre **p**, because while **Point3d** (the class in which the references to fields **x** and **y** occur) is a subclass of **Point** (the class in which **x** and **y** are declared), it is not involved in the implementation of a **Point** (the type of the parametre **p**). The method **delta3d** can access the protected members of its parametre **q**, because the class **Point3d** is a subclass of **Point** and is involved in the implementation of a **Point3d**. The method **delta** could try to cast its parametre to be a **Point3d**, but this cast would fail, causing an exception, if the class of **p** at run time were not **Point3d**. A compile-time error also occurs in the method warp: it cannot access the protected member **z** of its parametre **a**, because while the class **Point** (the class in which the reference to field **z** occurs) is involved in the implementation of a **Point3d** (the type of the parametre **a**), it is not a subclass of **Point3d** (the class in which **z** is declared).

PRIVATE FIELDS, METHODS, AND CONSTRUCTORS

A **private** class member or constructor is accessible only within the body of the top level class that encloses the declaration of the member or constructor. It is not inherited by subclasses. In the example:

```
class Point {
    Point() { setMasterID(); }
    int x, y;
    private int ID;
    private static int masterID = 0;
    private void setMasterID() { ID =
    masterID++; }
}
```

the `private` members `ID`, `masterID`, and `setMasterID` may be used only within the body of class `Point`. They may not be accessed by qualified names, field access expressions, or method invocation expressions outside the body of the declaration of `Point`.

FULLY QUALIFIED NAMES AND CANONICAL NAMES

Every package, top level class, top level interface, and primitive type has a *fully qualified name.* An array type has a fully qualified name if and only if its element type has a fully qualified name.

- The fully qualified name of a primitive type is the keyword for that primitive type, namely boolean, char, byte, short, int, long, float, or double.
- The fully qualified name of a named package that is not a subpackage of a named package is its simple name.
- The fully qualified name of a named package that is a subpackage of another named package consists of the fully qualified name of the containing package, followed by ".", followed by the simple (member) name of the subpackage.
- The fully qualified name of a top level class or top level interface that is declared in an unnamed package is the simple name of the class or interface.
- The fully qualified name of a top level class or top level interface that is declared in a named package consists of the fully qualified name of the package, followed by ".", followed by the simple name of the class or interface.
- A member class or member interface *M* of another class C has a fully qualified name if and only if C has a fully qualified name. In that case, the fully qualified name of *M* consists of the fully qualified name of C, followed by ".", followed by the simple name of *M*.
- The fully qualified name of an array type consists of the fully qualified name of the component type of the array type followed by "[]".

Examples:

- The fully qualified name of the type long is "long".
- The fully qualified name of the package java.lang is "java.lang" because it is subpackage lang of package java.
- The fully qualified name of the class Object, which is defined in the package java.lang, is "java.lang.Object".
- The fully qualified name of the interface Enumeration, which is defined in the package java.util, is "java.util.Enumeration".
- The fully qualified name of the type "array of double" is "double[]".
- The fully qualified name of the type "array of array of array of array of String" is "java.lang.String [][][][]".

In the example:

```
   package points;
class Point { int x, y; }
class PointVec {
   Point[] vec;
}
```

the fully qualified name of the type **Point** is "**points.Point**"; the fully qualified name of the type **PointVec** is "**points.PointVec**"; and the fully qualified name of the type of the field **vec** of class **PointVec** is "**points.Point[]**". Every package, top level class, top level interface, and primitive type has a *canonical name.*

An array type has a canonical name if and only if its element type has a canonical name. A member class or member interface *M* declared in another class C has a canonical name if and only if C has a canonical name. In that case, the canonical name of *M* consists of the canonical name of C, followed by ".", followed by the simple name of *M*. For every package, top level class, top level interface and primitive type, the canonical name is the same as the fully qualified name. The canonical name of an array type is defined only when the component type of the array has a canonical name. In that case, the canonical name of the array type consists of the canonical name of the component type of the array type followed by "`[]`".

The difference between a fully qualified name and a canonical name can be seen in examples such as:

```
package p;
class O1 { class I{}}
class O2 extends O1{};
```

In this example both **p.O1.I** and **p.O2.I** are fully qualified names that denote the same class, but only **p.O1.I** is its canonical name.

NAMING CONVENTIONS

The class libraries of the Java platform attempt to use, whenever possible, names chosen according to the conventions presented here. These conventions help to make code more readable and avoid certain kinds of name conflicts. We recommend these conventions for use in all programs written in the Java programming language.

However, these conventions should not be followed slavishly if long-held conventional usage dictates otherwise. So, for example, the **sin** and **cos** methods of the class **java.lang.Math** have mathematically conventional names, even though these method names flout the convention suggested here because they are short and are not verbs.

PACKAGE NAMES

Names of packages that are to be made widely available should be formed as described in. Such names are always qualified names whose first identifier consists of two or three lowercase letters that name an Internet domain, such as **com**, **edu**, **gov**, **mil**, **net**, **org**, or a two-letter ISO country code such as **uk** or **jp**. Here are examples of hypothetical unique names that might be formed under this convention:

```
com.JavaSoft.jag.Oak
org.npr.pledge.driver
uk.ac.city.rugby.game
```

Names of packages intended only for local use should have a first identifier that begins with a lowercase letter, but that first identifier specifically should not be the identifier **java**;

package names that start with the identifier **java** are reserved by Sun for naming Java platform packages.

When package names occur in expressions:

- If a package name is obscured by a field declaration, then import declarations can usually be used to make available the type names declared in that package.
- If a package name is obscured by a declaration of a parametre or local variable, then the name of the parametre or local variable can be changed without affecting other code.

The first component of a package name is normally not easily mistaken for a type name, as a type name normally begins with a single uppercase letter. (The Java programming language does not actually rely on case distinctions to determine whether a name is a package name or a type name.)

CLASS AND INTERFACE TYPE NAMES

Names of class types should be descriptive nouns or noun phrases, not overly long, in mixed case with the first letter of each word capitalized. For example:

ClassLoader
SecurityManager
Thread
Dictionary
BufferedInputStream

Likewise, names of interface types should be short and descriptive, not overly long, in mixed case with the first letter of each word capitalized. The name may be a descriptive noun or noun phrase, which is appropriate when an interface is used as if it were an abstract superclass, such as interfaces **java.io.DataInput** and **java.io.DataOutput**; or it may be an adjective describing a behaviour, as for the interfaces **Runnable** and **Cloneable**.

Obscuring involving class and interface type names is rare. Names of fields, parametres, and local variables normally do not obscure type names because they conventionally begin with a lowercase letter whereas type names conventionally begin with an uppercase letter.

TYPE VARIABLE NAMES

Type variable names should be pithy (single character if possible) yet evocative, and should not include lower case letters. Discussion: This makes it easy to distinguish formal type parametres from ordinary classes and interfaces. Container types should use the name **`E`** for their element type. Maps should use **`K`** for the type of their keys and **`V`** for the type of their values. The name **`X`** should be used for arbitrary exception types. We use **`T`** for type, whenever there isn't anything more specific about the type to distinguish it.

Discussion: This is often the case in generic methods.

If there are multiple type parametres that denote arbitrary types, one should use letters that neighbour **`T`** in the alphabet, such as **`S`**. Alternately, it is acceptable to use numeric subscripts (*e.g.*, **`T1, T2`**) to distinguish among the different type variables. In such cases, all the variables with the same prefix should be subscripted.

Discussion: If a generic method appears inside a generic class, it's a good idea to avoid using the same names for the type parametres of the method and class, to avoid confusion. The same applies to nested generic classes.

Discussion: These conventions are illustrated in the code snippets below:

```
public class HashSet<E> extends AbstractSet<E> {... }
public class HashMap<K,V> extends AbstractMap<K,V> {... }
public class ThreadLocal<T> {... }
public interface Functor<T, X extends Throwable> {
    T eval() throws X;
}
```

When type parametres do not fall conveniently into one of the categories mentioned, names should be chosen to be as meaningful as possible within the confines of a single letter. The names mentioned above (**`E, K, T, V, X`**) should not be used for type parametres that do not fall into the designated categories.

METHOD NAMES

Method names should be verbs or verb phrases, in mixed case, with the first letter lowercase and the first letter of any subsequent words capitalized. Here are some additional specific conventions for method names:

- Methods to get and set an attribute that might be thought of as a variable *V* should be named get*V* and set*V*. An example is the methods getPriority and setPriority of class Thread.
- A method that returns the length of something should be named length, as in class String.
- A method that tests a boolean condition *V* about an object should be named is*V*. An example is the method isInterrupted of class Thread.
- A method that converts its object to a particular format *F* should be named to*F*. Examples are the method toString of class Object and the methods toLocaleString and toGMTString of class java.util.Date.

Whenever possible and appropriate, basing the names of methods in a new class on names in an existing class that is similar, especially a class from the Java Application Programming Interface classes, will make it easier to use. Method names cannot obscure or be obscured by other names.

FIELD NAMES

Names of fields that are not final should be in mixed case with a lowercase first letter and the first letters of subsequent words capitalized. Note that well-designed classes have very few public or protected fields, except for fields that are constants (final static fields). Fields should have names that are nouns, noun phrases, or abbreviations for nouns. Examples of this convention are the fields buf, pos, and count of the class java. io. Byte Array Input Stream and the field bytesTransferred of the class java.io.Interrupted IO Exception.

Obscuring involving field names is rare:

- If a field name obscures a package name, then an import declaration can usually be used to make available the type names declared in that package.

- If a field name obscures a type name, then a fully qualified name for the type can be used unless the type name denotes a local class.
- Field names cannot obscure method names.
- If a field name is shadowed by a declaration of a parametre or local variable, then the name of the parametre or local variable can be changed without affecting other code.

CONSTANT NAMES

The names of constants in interface types should be, and `final` variables of class types may conventionally be, a sequence of one or more words, acronyms, or abbreviations, all uppercase, with components separated by underscore "_" characters.

Constant names should be descriptive and not unnecessarily abbreviated. Conventionally they may be any appropriate part of speech. Examples of names for constants include `MIN_VALUE`, `MAX_VALUE`, `MIN_RADIX`, and `MAX_RADIX` of the class `Character`.

A group of constants that represent alternative values of a set, or, less frequently, masking bits in an integer value, are sometimes usefully specified with a common acronym as a name prefix, as in:

```
interface ProcessStates {
        int PS_RUNNING = 0;
        int PS_SUSPENDED = 1;
}
```

Obscuring involving constant names is rare:

- Constant names normally have no lowercase letters, so they will not normally obscure names of packages or types, nor will they normally shadow fields, whose names typically contain at least one lowercase letter.
- Constant names cannot obscure method names, because they are distinguished syntactically.

LOCAL VARIABLE AND PARAMETRE NAMES

Local variable and parametre names should be short, yet

meaningful. They are often short sequences of lowercase letters that are not words.

For example:

- Acronyms, that is the first letter of a series of words, as in cp for a variable holding a reference to a ColoredPoint
- Abbreviations, as in buf holding a pointer to a buffer of some kind
- Mnemonic terms, organized in some way to aid memory and understanding, typically by using a set of local variables with conventional names patterned after the names of parametres to widely used classes. For example:
  - In and out, whenever some kind of input and output are involved, patterned after the fields of System
  - Off and len, whenever an offset and length are involved, patterned after the parametres to the read and write methods of the interfaces DataInput and DataOutput of java.io

One-character local variable or parametre names should be avoided, except for temporary and looping variables, or where a variable holds an undistinguished value of a type.

Conventional one-character names are:

- b for a byte
- c for a char
- d for a double
- e for an Exception
- f for a float
- i, j, and k for integers
- l for a long
- o for an Object
- s for a String
- v for an arbitrary value of some type

Local variable or parametre names that consist of only two or three lowercase letters should not conflict with the initial country codes and domain names that are the first component of unique package names.

4

Packages

INTRODUCTION

Programs are organized as sets of packages. Each package has its own set of names for types, which helps to prevent name conflicts. A top level type is accessible outside the package that declares it only if the type is declared `public`. The naming structure for packages is hierarchical.

The members of a package are class and interface types, which are declared in compilation units of the package, and subpackages, which may contain compilation units and subpackages of their own. A package can be stored in a file system or in a database.

Packages that are stored in a file system may have certain constraints on the organization of their compilation units to allow a simple implementation to find classes easily. A package consists of a number of compilation units. A compilation unit automatically has access to all types declared in its package and also automatically imports all of the public types declared in the predefined package `java.lang`.

For small programs and casual development, a package can be unnamed or have a simple name, but if code is to be widely distributed, unique package names should be chosen.This can prevent the conflicts that would otherwise occur if two development groups happened to pick the same package name and these packages were later to be used in a single program.

PACKAGE MEMBERS

The members of a package are its subpackages and all the

top level class types and top level interface types declared in all the compilation units of the package.

For example, in the Java Application Programming Interface:

- The package **java** has subpackages **awt, applet, io, lang, net**, and **util**, but no compilation units.
- The package **java.awt** has a subpackage named **image**, as well as a number of compilation units containing declarations of class and interface types.

If the fully qualified name of a package is *P*, and *Q* is a subpackage of *P*, then *P.Q* is the fully qualified name of the subpackage.

A package may not contain two members of the same name, or a compile-time error results.

Here are some examples:

- Because the package **java.awt** has a subpackage **image**, it cannot (and does not) contain a declaration of a class or interface type named **image**.
- If there is a package named **mouse** and a member type **Button** in that package (which then might be referred to as **mouse.Button**), then there cannot be any package with the fully qualified name **mouse.Button** or **mouse.Button.Click**.
- If **com.sun.java.jag** is the fully qualified name of a type, then there cannot be any package whose fully qualified name is either **com.sun.java.jag** or **com.sun.java.jag.scrabble**.

The hierarchical naming structure for packages is intended to be convenient for organizing related packages in a conventional manner, but has no significance in itself other than the prohibition against a package having a subpackage with the same simple name as a top level type declared in that package.

There is no special access relationship between a package named `oliver` and another package named `oliver.twist`, or between packages named `evelyn.wood` and `evelyn.waugh`. For example, the code in a package named `oliver.twist` has no better access to the types declared within package `oliver` than code in any other package.

HOST SUPPORT FOR PACKAGES

Each host determines how packages, compilation units, and subpackages are created and stored, and which compilation units are observable in a particular compilation. The observability of compilation units in turn determines which packages are observable, and which packages are in scope. The packages may be stored in a local file system in simple implementations of the Java platform. Other implementations may use a distributed file system or some form of database to store source and/or binary code.

STORING PACKAGES IN A FILE SYSTEM

As an extremely simple example, all the packages and source and binary code on a system might be stored in a single directory and its subdirectories. Each immediate subdirectory of this directory would represent a top level package, that is, one whose fully qualified name consists of a single simple name. The directory might contain the following immediate subdirectories:

```
com
gls
jag
java
wnj
```

where directory `java` would contain the Java Application Programming Interface packages; the directories `jag`, `gls`, and `wnj` might contain packages that three of the authors of this specification created for their personal use and to share with each other within this small group; and the directory `com` would contain packages procured from companies that used the conventions described in to generate unique names for their packages.

Continuing the example, the directory `java` *would contain, among others, the following subdirectories*:

```
applet
awt
io
lang
```

```
net
util
```

corresponding to the packages **java.applet**, **java.awt**, **java.io**, **java.lang**, **java.net**, and **java.util** that are defined as part of the Java Application Programming Interface.

Still continuing the example, if we were to look inside the directory **util**, we might see the following files:

```
BitSet.java        Observable.java
BitSet.class       Observable.class
Date.java          Observer.java
Date.class         Observer.class
...
```

where each of the.**java** files contains the source for a compilation unit that contains the definition of a class or interface whose binary compiled form is contained in the corresponding.**class** file.

Under this simple organization of packages, an implementation of the Java platform would transform a package name into a pathname by concatenating the components of the package name, placing a file name separator (directory indicator) between adjacent components. For example, if this simple organization were used on a UNIX system, where the file name separator is /, the package name:

```
jag.scrabble.board
```

would be transformed into the directory name:

```
jag/scrabble/board
```

and:

```
com.sun.sunsoft.DOE
```

would be transformed to the directory name:

com/sun/sunsoft/DOE

A package name component or class name might contain a character that cannot correctly appear in a host file system's ordinary directory name, such as a Unicode character on a system that allows only ASCII characters in file names. As a convention, the character can be escaped by using, say, the @ character followed by four hexadecimal digits giving the numeric value of the character, as in the \u*xxxx* escape, so that the package name:

children.activities.crafts.papierM\u00e2ch\u00e9

which can also be written using full Unicode as:

children.activities.crafts.papierMâché

might be mapped to the directory name:

children/activities/crafts/papierM@00e2ch@00e9

If the @ character is not a valid character in a file name for some given host file system, then some other character that is not valid in a identifier could be used instead.

STORING PACKAGES IN A DATABASE

A host system may store packages and their compilation units and subpackages in a database. Such a database must not impose the optional restrictions on compilation units in file-based implementations.

For example, a system that uses a database to store packages may not enforce a maximum of one `public` class or interface per compilation unit. Systems that use a database must, however, provide an option to convert a program to a form that obeys the restrictions, for purposes of export to file-based implementations.

COMPILATION UNITS

CompilationUnit is the goal symbol for the syntactic grammar of Java programs. It is defined by the following productions:

```
CompilationUnit:
    PackageDeclarationopt ImportDeclarationsopt
    TypeDeclarationsopt
ImportDeclarations:
    ImportDeclaration
    ImportDeclarations  ImportDeclaration
TypeDeclarations:
    TypeDeclaration
    TypeDeclarations  TypeDeclaration
```

Types declared in different compilation units can depend on each other, circularly. A Java compiler must arrange to compile all such types at the same time.

A *compilation unit* consists of three parts, each of which is optional:

- A package declaration, giving the fully qualified name of the package to which the compilation unit belongs. A compilation unit that has no package declaration is part of an unnamed package.
- Import declarations that allow types from other packages and static members of types to be referred to using their simple names
- Top level type declarations of class and interface types

Which compilation units are *observable* is determined by the host system. However, all the compilation units of the package java and its subpackages lang and io must always be observable. The observability of a compilation unit influences the observability of its package.

Every compilation unit automatically and implicitly imports every public type name declared by the predefined package java.lang, so that the names of all those types are available as simple names.

PACKAGE DECLARATIONS

A package declaration appears within a compilation unit to indicate the package to which the compilation unit belongs.

NAMED PACKAGES

A *package declaration* in a compilation unit specifies the name of the package to which the compilation unit belongs.

```
PackageDeclaration:
    Annotationsopt package PackageName ;
```

The keyword **package** may optionally be preceded by annotation modifiers.If an annotation *a* on a package declaration corresponds to an annotation type *T*, and *T* has a (meta-)annotation *m* that corresponds to **annotation .Target**, then *m* must have an element whose value is **annotation.ElementType.PACKAGE**, or a compile-time error occurs. The package name mentioned in a package declaration must be the fully qualified name of the package.

PACKAGE ANNOTATIONS

Annotations may be used on package declarations, with the restriction that at most one annotated package declaration is permitted for a given package. Discussion: The manner in which this restriction is enforced must, of necessity, vary from implementation to implementation. The following scheme is strongly recommended for file-system-based implementations: The sole annotated package declaration, if it exists, is placed in a source file called `package-info.java` in the directory containing the source files for the package.

This file does not contain the source for a class called package-info.java; indeed it would be illegal for it to do so, as package-info is not a legal identifier. Typically `package-info.java` contains only a package declaration, preceded immediately by the annotations on the package. While the file could technically contain the source code for one or more package-private classes, it would be very bad form. It is recommended that `package-info.java`, if it is present, take the place of `package.html` for javadoc and other similar documentation generation systems.

If this file is present, the documentation generation tool should look for the package documentation comment immediately preceding the (possibly annotated) package declaration in `package-info.java`. In this way, package-info.java becomes the sole repository for package level annotations and documentation. If, in future, it becomes desirable to add any other package-level information, this file should prove a convenient home for this information.

UNNAMED PACKAGES

A compilation unit that has no package declaration is part of an unnamed package. Note that an unnamed package cannot have subpackages, since the syntax of a package declaration always includes a reference to a named top level package.

```
As an example, the compilation unit:
class FirstCall {
    public static void main(String[] args) {
    System.out.println("Mr. Watson, come here.
```

```
    "
    + "I want you.");
    }
}
```

defines a very simple compilation unit as part of an unnamed package. An implementation of the Java platform must support at least one unnamed package; it may support more than one unnamed package but is not required to do so. Which compilation units are in each unnamed package is determined by the host system.

In implementations of the Java platform that use a hierarchical file system for storing packages, one typical strategy is to associate an unnamed package with each directory; only one unnamed package is observable at a time, namely the one that is associated with the "current working directory." The precise meaning of "current working directory" depends on the host system.

Unnamed packages are provided by the Java platform principally for convenience when developing small or temporary applications or when just beginning development.

OBSERVABILITY OF A PACKAGE

A package is observable if and only if either:

- A compilation unit containing a declaration of the package is observable.
- A subpackage of the package is observable.

One can conclude from the rule above and from the requirements on observable compilation units, that the packages `java`, `java.lang`, and `java.io` are always observable.

SCOPE OF A PACKAGE DECLARATION

The scope of the declaration of an observable top level package is all observable compilation units. The declaration of a package that is not observable is never in scope. Subpackage declarations are never in scope.It follows that the package `java` is always in scope.Package declarations never shadow other declarations.

IMPORT DECLARATIONS

An *import declaration* allows a static member or a named type to be referred to by a simple name that consists of a single identifier. Without the use of an appropriate **`import`** declaration, the only way to refer to a type declared in another package, or a static member of another type, is to use a fully qualified name.

```
ImportDeclaration:
    SingleTypeImportDeclaration
    TypeImportOnDemandDeclaration
    SingleStaticImportDeclaration
    StaticImportOnDemandDeclaration
```

A single-type-import declaration imports a single named type, by mentioning its canonical name. A type-import-on-demand declaration imports all the accessible types of a named type or package as needed. It is a compile time error to import a type from the unnamed package. A single static import declaration imports all accessible static members with a given name from a type, by giving its canonical name.

A static-import-on-demand declaration imports all accessible static members of a named type as needed. The scope of a type imported by a single-type-import declaration or a type-import-on-demand declaration is all the class and interface type declarations in the compilation unit in which the import declaration appears.

The scope of a member imported by a single-static-import declaration or a static-import-on-demand declaration is all the class and interface type declarations in the compilation unit in which the import declaration appears. An `import` declaration makes types available by their simple names only within the compilation unit that actually contains the `import` declaration.

The scope of the entities(s) it introduces specifically does not include the **`package`** statement, other `import` declarations in the current compilation unit, or other compilation units in the same package.

SINGLE-TYPE-IMPORT DECLARATION

A *single-type-import declaration* imports a single type by giving its canonical name, making it available under a simple name in the class and interface declarations of the compilation unit in which the single-type import declaration appears.

```
SingleTypeImportDeclaration:
    import TypeName ;
```

The *TypeName* must be the canonical name of a class or interface type; a compile-time error occurs if the named type does not exist. The named type must be accessible or a compile-time error occurs.

A single-type-import declaration *d* in a compilation unit *c* of package *p* that imports a type named *n* shadows the declarations of:

- Any top level type named *n* declared in another compilation unit of *p*.
- Any type named *n* imported by a type-import-on-demand declaration in *c*.
- Any type named *n* imported by a static-import-on-demand declaration in *c*.

`throughout c.`

The example:

```
import java.util.Vector;
```

causes the simple name `Vector` to be available within the class and interface declarations in a compilation unit. Thus, the simple name `Vector` refers to the type declaration `Vector` in the package `java.util` in all places where it is not shadowed or obscured by a declaration of a field, parametre, local variable, or nested type declaration with the same name.

Discussion: Note that `Vector` is declared as a generic type. Once imported, the name `Vector` can be used without qualification in a parametreized type such as `Vector <String>`, or as the raw type `Vector.`

This highlights a limitation of the `import` declaration. A type nested inside a generic type declaration can be imported, but its outer type is always erased. If two single-type-import declarations in the same compilation unit attempt to import types with the same simple name, then a compile-time error occurs, unless the two types are the same type, in which case the duplicate declaration is ignored. If the type imported by the the single-type-import declaration is declared in the compilation unit that contains the import declaration, the import declaration is ignored.

If a compilation unit contains both a single-static-import declaration that imports a type whose simple name is *n*, and a single-type-import declaration that imports a type whose simple name is *n*, a compile-time error occurs. If another top level type with the same simple name is otherwise declared in the current compilation unit except by a type-import-on-demand declaration or a static-import-on-demand declaration, then a compile-time error occurs.

So the sample program:

```
import java.util.Vector;
class Vector { Object[] vec; }
```

causes a compile-time error because of the duplicate declaration of `Vector`, as does:

```
import java.util.Vector;
import myVector.Vector;
```

where `myVector` is a package containing the compilation unit:

```
package myVector;
public class Vector { Object[] vec; }
```

The compiler keeps track of types by their binary names.

Note that an import statement cannot import a subpackage, only a type. For example, it does not work to try to import `java.util` and then use the name `util.Random` to refer to the type `java.util.Random`:

```
import java.util; // incorrect: compile-time
error
class Test { util.Random generator; }
```

TYPE-IMPORT-ON-DEMAND DECLARATION

A *type-import-on-demand declaration* allows all accessible types declared in the type or package named by a canonical name to be imported as needed.

```
TypeImportOnDemandDeclaration:
    import PackageOrTypeName . * ;
```

It is a compile-time error for a type-import-on-demand declaration to name a type or package that is not accessible.

Two or more type-import-on-demand declarations in the same compilation unit may name the same type or package. All but one of these declarations are considered *redundant*; the effect is as if that type was imported only once. If a compilation unit contains both a static-import-on-demand declaration and a type-import-on-demand declaration that name the same type, the effect is as if the static member types of that type were imported only once. It is not a compile-time error to name the current package or `java.lang` in a type-import-on-demand declaration. The type-import-on-demand declaration is ignored in such cases.

A type-import-on-demand declaration never causes any other declaration to be shadowed.

The example:

```
import java.util.*;
```

causes the simple names of all `public` types declared in the package `java.util` to be available within the class and interface declarations of the compilation unit. Thus, the simple name `Vector` refers to the type `Vector` in the package `java.util` in all places in the compilation unit where that type declaration is not shadowed or obscured. The declaration might be shadowed by a single-type-import declaration of a type whose simple name is `Vector`; by a type named `Vector` and declared in the package to which the compilation unit belongs; or any nested classes or interfaces. The declaration might be obscured by a declaration of a field, parametre, or local variable named `Vector` (It would be unusual for any of these conditions to occur.)

Single Static Import Declaration

A *single-static-import declaration* imports all accessible static members with a given simple name from a type.

This makes these static members available under their simple name in the class and interface declarations of the compilation unit in which the single-static import declaration appears.

```
SingleStaticImportDeclaration:
    import static TypeName. Identifier;
```

The *TypeName* must be the canonical name of a class or interface type; a compile-time error occurs if the named type does not exist. The named type must be accessible or a compile-time error occurs. The Identifier must name at least one static member of the named type; a compile-time error occurs if there is no member of that name or if all of the named members are not accessible.

A single-static-import declaration *d* in a compilation unit *c* of package *p* that imports a field named *n* shadows the declaration of any static field named *n* imported by a static-import-on-demand declaration in *c*, throughout *c*.

A single-static-import declaration *d* in a compilation unit *c* of package *p* that imports a method named *n* with signature s shadows the declaration of any static method named *n* with signature *s* imported by a static-import-on-demand declaration in *c*, throughout *c*. A single-static-import declaration *d* in a compilation unit *c* of package *p* that imports a type named *n* shadows the declarations of:

- Any static type named *n* imported by a static-import-on-demand declaration in *c*.
- Any top level type named *n* declared in another compilation unit of *p*.
- Any type named *n* imported by a type-import-on-demand declaration in *c*.

`throughout c.`

Note that it is permissable for one single-static-import declaration to import several fields or types with the same name, or several methods with the same name and signature. If a compilation unit contains both a single-static-import declaration that imports a type whose simple name is *n*, and a single-type-import declaration that imports a type whose simple name is *n*, a compile-time error occurs. If a single-static-import declaration imports a type whose simple name is *n*, and the compilation unit also declares a top level type whose simple name is *n*, a compile-time error occurs.

STATIC-IMPORT-ON-DEMAND DECLARATION

A *static-import-on-demand declaration* allows all accessible static members declared in the type named by a canonical name to be imported as needed.

```
StaticImportOnDemandDeclaration:
      import static TypeName. * ;
```

It is a compile-time error for a static-import-on-demand declaration to name a type that does not exist or a type that is not accessible. Two or more static-import-on-demand declarations in the same compilation unit may name the same type or package; the effect is as if there was exactly one such declaration. Two or more static-import-on-demand declarations in the same compilation unit may name the same member; the effect is as if the member was imported exactly once.

Note that it is permissable for one static-import-on-demand declaration to import several fields or types with the same name, or several methods with the same name and signature. If a compilation unit contains both a static-import-on-demand declaration and a type-import-on-demand declaration that name the same type, the effect is as if the static member types of that type were imported only once. A static-import-on-demand declaration never causes any other declaration to be shadowed.

AUTOMATIC IMPORTS

Each compilation unit automatically imports all of the public type names declared in the predefined package java.lang, as if the declaration:

```
import java.lang.*;
```

appeared at the beginning of each compilation unit, immediately following any **package** statement.

A STRANGE EXAMPLE

Package names and type names are usually different under the naming conventions. Nevertheless, in a contrived example where there is an unconventionally-named package **Vector**, which declares a **public** class whose

```
name is Mosquito:
package Vector;
```

```
public class Mosquito { int capacity; }
```

and then the compilation unit:

```
package strange.example;
import java.util.Vector;
import Vector.Mosquito;
class Test {
    public static void main(String[] args) {
        System.out.println(new
    Vector().getClass());
        System.out.println(new
    Mosquito().getClass());
    }
}
```

the single-type-import declaration importing class `Vector` from package `java.util` does not prevent the package name `Vector` from appearing and being correctly recognized in subsequent `import` declarations. The example compiles and produces the output:

```
class java.util.Vector
class Vector.Mosquito
```

TOP LEVEL TYPE DECLARATIONS

A *top level type declaration* declares a top level class type or a top level interface type:

```
TypeDeclaration:
    ClassDeclaration
    InterfaceDeclaration
    ;
```

By default, the top level types declared in a package are accessible only within the compilation units of that package, but a type may be declared to be `public` to grant access to the type from code in other packages.

The scope of a top level type is all type declarations in the package in which the top level type is declared. If a top level type named *T* is declared in a compilation unit of a package whose fully qualified name is *P*, then the fully qualified name of the type is *P.T*. If the type is declared in an unnamed package, then the type has the fully qualified name *T*.

Thus in the example:

```
package wnj.points;
class Point { int x, y; }
```

the fully qualified name of class `Point` is `wnj.points.Point`.

An implementation of the Java platform must keep track of types within packages by their binary names. Multiple ways of naming a type must be expanded to binary names to make sure that such names are understood as referring to the same type.

For example, if a compilation unit contains the single-type-import declaration:

```
import java.util.Vector;
```

then within that compilation unit the simple name `Vector` and the fully qualified name `java.util.Vector` refer to the same type.

When packages are stored in a file system, the host system may choose to enforce the restriction that it is a compile-time error if a type is not found in a file under a name composed of the type name plus an extension (such as.`java` or.`jav`) if either of the following is true:

- The type is referred to by code in other compilation units of the package in which the type is declared.
- The type is declared public (and therefore is potentially accessible from code in other packages).

This restriction implies that there must be at most one such type per compilation unit. This restriction makes it easy for a compiler for the Java programming language or an implementation of the Java virtual machine to find a named class within a package; for example, the source code for a `public` type `wet.sprocket.Toad` would be found in a file `Toad.java` in the directory `wet/sprocket`, and the corresponding object code would be found in the file `Toad.class` in the same directory.

When packages are stored in a database, the host system must not impose such restrictions. In practice, many programmers choose to put each class or interface type in its own compilation unit, whether or not it is public or is referred to by code in other compilation units. A compile-time error occurs if the name of a top level type appears as the name of any other top level class or interface type declared in the same package.

A compile-time error occurs if the name of a top level type is also declared as a type by a single-type-import declaration in the compilation unit containing the type declaration.

In the example:

```
class Point { int x, y; }
```

the class Point is declared in a compilation unit with no package statement, and thus Point is its fully qualified name, whereas in the example:

```
package vista;
class Point { int x, y; }
```

the fully qualified name of the class Point is `vista.Point`. (The package name vista is suitable for local or personal use; if the package were intended to be widely distributed, it would be better to give it a unique package name.)

In the example:

```
package test;
import java.util.Vector;
class Point {
    int x, y;
}
interface Point {
// compile-time error #1
    int getR();
    int getTheta();
}
class Vector { Point[] pts; }
// compile-time error #2
```

the first compile-time error is caused by the duplicate declaration of the name Point as both a class and an `interface` in the same package. A second error detected at compile time is the attempt to declare the name Vector both by a class type declaration and by a single-type-import declaration. Note, however, that it is not an error for the name of a class to also to name a type that otherwise might be imported by a type-import-on-demand declaration in the compilation unit containing the class declaration. In the example:

```
   package test;
   import java.util.*;
   class Vector { Point[] pts; }
// not a compile-time error
```

the declaration of the class `Vector` is permitted even though there is also a class `java.util.Vector`. Within this compilation unit, the simple name `Vector` refers to the class `test.Vector`, not to `java.util.Vector` (which can still be referred to by code within the compilation unit, but only by its fully qualified name).

As another example, the compilation unit:

```
package points;
class Point {
    int x, y; // coordinates
    PointColor color; // color of this point
    Point next; // next point with this color
    static int nPoints;
}
class PointColor {
    Point first; // first point with this color
    PointColor(int color) {
         this.color = color;
    }
    private int color;      // color components
}
```

defines two classes that use each other in the declarations of their class members. Because the class types `Point` and `PointColor` have all the type declarations in package points, including all those in the current compilation unit, as their scope, this example compiles correctly-that is, forward reference is not a problem. It is a compile-time error if a top level type declaration contains any one of the following access modifiers: `protected`, `private` or `static`.

UNIQUE PACKAGE NAMES

Developers should take steps to avoid the possibility of

two published packages having the same name by choosing *unique package names* for packages that are widely distributed. This allows packages to be easily and automatically installed and catalogued. This section specifies a suggested convention for generating such unique package names. Implementations of the Java platform are encouraged to provide automatic support for converting a set of packages from local and casual package names to the unique name format described here.

If unique package names are not used, then package name conflicts may arise far from the point of creation of either of the conflicting packages. This may create a situation that is difficult or impossible for the user or programmer to resolve. The class **ClassLoader** can be used to isolate packages with the same name from each other in those cases where the packages will have constrained interactions, but not in a way that is transparent to a naïve program.

You form a unique package name by first having (or belonging to an organization that has) an Internet domain name, such as **sun.com**. You then reverse this name, component by component, to obtain, in this example, **com.sun**, and use this as a prefix for your package names, using a convention developed within your organization to further administer package names.

In some cases, the internet domain name may not be a valid package name. Here are some suggested conventions for dealing with these situations:

- If the domain name contains a hyphen, or any other special character not allowed in an identifier, convert it into an underscore.
- If any of the resulting package name components are keywords then append underscore to them.
- If any of the resulting package name components start with a digit, or any other character that is not allowed as an initial character of an identifier, have an underscore prefixed to the component.

Such a convention might specify that certain directory name components be division, department, project, machine, or login names. Some possible examples:

```
com.sun.sunsoft.DOE
com.sun.java.jag.scrabble
com.apple.quicktime.v2
edu.cmu.cs.bovik.cheese
gov.whitehouse.socks.mousefinder
```

The first component of a unique package name is always written in all-lowercase ASCII letters and should be one of the top level domain names, currently **com**, **edu**, **gov**, **mil**, **net**, **org**, or one of the English two-letter codes identifying countries as specified in ISO Standard 3166, 1981. For more information, refer to the documents stored at **ftp://rs.internic.net/rfc**, for example, **rfc920.txt** and **rfc1032.txt**.

The name of a package is not meant to imply where the package is stored within the Internet; for example, a package named **edu.cmu.cs.bovik.cheese** is not necessarily obtainable from Internet address **cmu.edu** or from **cs.cmu.edu** or from **bovik.cs.cmu.edu**. The suggested convention for generating unique package names is merely a way to piggyback a package naming convention on top of an existing, widely known unique name registry instead of having to create a separate registry for package names.

5

Class Declaration

BACKGROUND

Class declarations define new reference types and describe how they are implemented. A *nested class* is any class whose declaration occurs within the body of another class or interface. A *top level class* is a class that is not a nested class. The common semantics of all classes-top level and nested (including member classes, local classes and anonymous classes).

Details that are specific to particular kinds of classes are discussed in the sections dedicated to these constructs. A named class may be declared abstract and must be declared abstract if it is incompletely implemented; such a class cannot be instantiated, but can be extended by subclasses. A class may be declared final, in which case it cannot have subclasses. If a class is declared public, then it can be referred to from other packages. Each class except Object is an extension of (that is, a subclass of) a single existing class and may implement interfaces. Classes may be generic, that is, they may declare type variables whose bindings may differ among different instances of the class.

Classes may be decorated with annotations just like any other kind of declaration. The body of a class declares members (fields and methods and nested classes and interfaces), instance and static initializers, and constructors.The scope of a member is the entire body of the declaration of the class to which the member belongs. Field, method, member class, member interface, and constructor declarations may include the access modifiers public, protected, or private. The members of a class include both declared and inherited members. Newly declared fields can hide fields declared in a superclass or superinterface. Newly declared class members and interface members can hide class or interface members declared in a superclass or superinterface.

Newly declared methods can hide, implement, or override methods declared in a superclass or superinterface. Field declarations describe class variables, which are incarnated once, and instance variables, which are freshly incarnated for each instance of the class. A field may be declared final, in which case it can be assigned to only once. Any field declaration may include an initializer.

Member class declarations describe nested classes that are members of the surrounding class. Member classes may be static, in which case they have no access to the instance variables of the surrounding class; or they may be inner classes. Member interface declarations describe nested interfaces that are members of the surrounding class.

Method declarations describe code that may be invoked by method invocation expressions.A class method is invoked relative to the class type; an instance method is invoked with respect to some particular object that is an instance of a class type. A method whose declaration does not indicate how it is implemented must be declared abstract. A method may be declared final, in which case it cannot be hidden or overridden. A method may be implemented by platform-dependent native code. A synchronized method automatically locks an object before executing its body and automatically unlocks the object on return, as if by use of a synchronized statement, thus allowing its activities to be synchronized with those of other threads.

Method names may be overloaded.Instance initializers are blocks of executable code that may be used to help initialize an instance when it is created.Static initializers are blocks of executable code that may be used to help initialize a class.Constructors are similar to methods, but cannot be invoked directly by a method call; they are used to initialize new class instances. Like methods, they may be overloaded.

CLASS DECLARATION

A *class declaration* specifies a new named reference type. There are two kinds of class declarations - *normal class declarations* and *enum declarations*:

```
ClassDeclaration:
    NormalClassDeclaration
    EnumDeclaration
NormalClassDeclaration:
    ClassModifiersopt class Identifier
    TypeParametresopt Superopt Interfacesopt
ClassBody
```

The rules in this section apply to all class declarations unless this specification explicitly states otherwise. In many cases, special restrictions apply to enum declarations.

The *Identifier* in a class declaration specifies the name of the class. A compile-time error occurs if a class has the same simple name as any of its enclosing classes or interfaces.

CLASS MODIFIERS

A class declaration may include *class modifiers*.

```
ClassModifiers:
    ClassModifier
    ClassModifiers ClassModifier
ClassModifier: one of
    Annotation public protected private
    abstract static final strictfp
```

Not all modifiers are applicable to all kinds of class declarations. The access modifier **`public`** pertains only to top level classes and to member classes, and is discussed in and. The access modifiers **`protected`** and **`private`** pertain only to member classes within a directly enclosing class declaration and are discussed in.The access modifier **`static`** pertains only to member classes. A compile-time error occurs if the same modifier appears more than once in a class declaration.

If an annotation *a* on a class declaration corresponds to an annotation type *T*, and *T* has a (meta-)annotation *m* that corresponds to **`annotation.Target`**, then *m* must have an element whose value is **`annotation.ElementType.TYPE`**, or a compile-time error occurs. Annotation modifiers are described later. If two or more class modifiers appear in a class declaration, then it is customary, though not required, that they appear in the order consistent with that shown above in the production for *ClassModifier*.

ABSTRACT CLASSES

An abstract class is a class that is incomplete, or to be considered incomplete. Normal classes may have abstract methods, that is methods that are declared but not yet implemented, only if they are abstract classes. If a normal class that is not abstract contains an abstract method, then a compile-time error occurs.

Enum types must not be declared abstract; doing so will result in a compile-time error. It is a compile-time error for an enum type *E* to have an abstract method *m* as a member unless *E* has one or more enum constants, and all of *E*'s enum constants have class bodies that provide concrete implementations of *m*. It is a compile-time error for the class body of an enum constant to declare an abstract method.

A class *C* has `abstract` methods if any of the following is true:

- C explicitly contains a declaration of an abstract method.
- Any of C's superclasses has an abstract method and C neither declares nor inherits a method that implements it.
- A direct superinterface of C declares or inherits a method (which is therefore necessarily abstract) and C neither declares nor inherits a method that implements it.

In the example:

```
abstract class Point {
    int x = 1, y = 1;
    void move(int dx, int dy) {
        x += dx;
        y += dy;
        alert();
```

```
    }
    abstract void alert();
}
abstract class ColoredPoint extends Point {
    int color;
}

class SimplePoint extends Point {
    void alert() { }
}
```

a class `Point` is declared that must be declared `abstract`, because it contains a declaration of an `abstract` method named `alert`. The subclass of `Point` named `ColoredPoint` inherits the `abstract` method `alert`, so it must also be declared `abstract`. On the other hand, the subclass of `Point` named `SimplePoint` provides an implementation of `alert`, so it need not be `abstract`.

A compile-time error occurs if an attempt is made to create an instance of an `abstract` class using a class instance creation expression.

Thus, continuing the example just shown, the statement:

```
Point p = new Point();
```

would result in a compile-time error; the class `Point` cannot be instantiated because it is `abstract`. However, a `Point` variable could correctly be initialized with a reference to any subclass of `Point`, and the class `SimplePoint` is not `abstract`, so the statement:

```
Point p = new SimplePoint();
```

would be correct.

A subclass of an `abstract` class that is not itself `abstract` may be instantiated, resulting in the execution of a constructor for the `abstract` class and, therefore, the execution of the field initializers for instance variables of that class. Thus, in the example just given, instantiation of a `SimplePoint` causes the default constructor and field initializers for `x` and `y` of `Point` to be executed. It is a compile-time error to declare an `abstract` class type such that it is not possible to create a subclass that implements all of its `abstract` methods. This situation can occur if the class would have as members two **abstract** methods that have the same method signature but incompatible return types.

As an example, the declarations:

```
interface Colorable { void setColor(int color);
   }
abstract class Colored implements Colorable {
    abstract int setColor(int color);
}
```

result in a compile-time error: it would be impossible for any subclass of class **Colored** to provide an implementation of a method named **setColor**, taking one argument of type **int**, that can satisfy both **abstract** method specifications, because the one in interface **Colorable** requires the same method to return no value, while the one in class **Colored** requires the same method to return a value of type **int**.

A class type should be declared **abstract** only if the intent is that subclasses can be created to complete the implementation. If the intent is simply to prevent instantiation of a class, the proper way to express this is to declare a constructor of no arguments, make it **private**, never invoke it, and declare no other constructors. A class of this form usually contains class methods and variables. The class **Math** is an example of a class that cannot be instantiated; its declaration looks like this:

```
public final class Math {
    private Math() { } // never instantiate
    this class
    ... declarations of class variables and
    methods...
}
```

FINAL CLASSES

A class can be declared **final** if its definition is complete and no subclasses are desired or required. A compile-time error occurs if the name of a **final** class appears in the **extends** clause of another **class** declaration; this implies that a **final** class cannot have any subclasses. A compile-time error occurs if a class is declared both **`final`** and **`abstract`**, because the implementation of such a class could never be completed. Because a **`final`** class never has any subclasses, the methods of a **`final`** class are never overridden.

STRICTFP CLASSES

The effect of the **`strictfp`** modifier is to make all **`float`** or **`double`** expressions within the class declaration be explicitly FP-strict.This implies that all methods declared in the class, and all nested types declared in the class, are implicitly strictfp.

Note also that all **`float`** or **`double`** expressions within all variable initializers, instance initializers, static initializers and constructors of the class will also be explicitly FP-strict.

Generic Classes and Type Parametres

A class is *generic* if it declares one or more type variables. These type variables are known as the *type parametres* of the class. The type parametre section follows the class name and is delimited by angle brackets. It defines one or more type variables that act as parametres. A generic class declaration defines a set of parametreized types, one for each possible invocation of the type parametre section. All of these parametreized types share the same class at runtime.

Discussion: For instance, executing the code

```
Vector<String> x = new Vector<String>();
Vector<Integer> y = new Vector<Integer>();
boolean b = x.getClass() == y.getClass();
```

will result in the variable **`b`** holding the value **`true`**.

```
TypeParametres ::= < TypeParametreList >
TypeParametreList    ::=  TypeParametreList  ,
    TypeParametre
                        |  TypeParametre
```

It is a compile-time error if a generic class is a direct or indirect subclass of **`Throwable`**.

Discussion: This restriction is needed since the **catch** mechanism of the Java virtual machine works only with non-generic classes.

The scope of a class' type parametre is the entire declaration of the class including the type parametre section itself. Therefore, type parametres can appear as parts of their own bounds, or as bounds of other type parametres declared in the same section.

It is a compile-time error to refer to a type parametre of a class C anywhere in the declaration of a static member of C or the declaration of a static member of any type declaration nested within C. It is a compile-time error to refer to a type parametre of a class C within a static initializer of C or any class nested within C.

Example: Mutually recursive type variable bounds.

```
interface ConvertibleTo<T> {
    T convert();
}
class ReprChange<T implements ConvertibleTo<S>,
    S implements ConvertibleTo<T>> {
    T t;
    void set(S s) {t = s.convert();}
    S get() {return t.convert();}
}
```

Parametreized class declarations can be nested inside other declarations.

Discussion: This is illustrated in the following example.

```
class Seq<T> {
    T head;
    Seq<T> tail;
    Seq() { this(null, null); }
    boolean isEmpty() { return tail == null; }
    Seq(T head, Seq<T> tail) { this.head = head;
    this.tail = tail; }
    class Zipper<S> {
        Seq<Pair<T,S>> zip(Seq<S> that) {
            if   (this.isEmpty()   ||
    that.isEmpty())
            return new Seq<Pair<T,S>>();
            else
            return new Seq<Pair<T,S>>(
```

```
                new Pair<T,S>(this.head,
    that.head),
            this.tail.zip(that.tail));
        }
    }
}
class Pair<T, S> {
    T fst; S Snd;
    Pair(T f, S s) {fst = f; snd = s;}
}
class Client {
    {
        Seq<String> strs =
        new     Seq<String>("a",     new
    Seq<String>("b",
            new Seq<String>()));
    Seq<Number> nums =
            new Seq<Number>(new Integer(1),
            new Seq<Number>(new Double(1.5),
            new Seq<Number>()));
    Seq<String>.Zipper<Number> zipper =
            strs.new Zipper<Number>();
    Seq<Pair<String,Number>> combined =
    zipper.zip(nums);
    }
}
```

INNER CLASSES AND ENCLOSING INSTANCES

An *inner class* is a nested class that is not explicitly or implicitly declared `static`. Inner classes may not declare static initializers or member interfaces. Inner classes may not declare static members, unless they are compile-time constant fields.

To illustrate these rules, consider the example below:

```
class HasStatic{
    static int j = 100;
}
class Outer{
    class Inner extends HasStatic{
```

```
        static final int x = 3; // ok - compile-
    time constant
        static int y = 4; // compile-time
    error, an inner class
    }
    static class NestedButNotInner{
    static int z = 5; // ok, not an inner class
    }
    interface NeverInner{}
    // interfaces are never inner
}
```

Inner classes may inherit static members that are not compile-time constants even though they may not declare them. Nested classes that are not inner classes may declare static members freely, in accordance with the usual rules of the Java programming language.

Member interfaces are always implicitly static so they are never considered to be inner classes. A statement or expression *occurs in a static context* if and only if the innermost method, constructor, instance initializer, static initializer, field initializer, or explicit constructor invocation statement enclosing the statement or expression is a static method, a static initializer, the variable initializer of a static variable, or an explicit constructor invocation statement.

An inner class C is a *direct inner class of a class O* if O is the immediately lexically enclosing class of C and the declaration of C does not occur in a static context. A class C is an *inner class of class O* if it is either a direct inner class of O or an inner class of an inner class of O.

A class O is the *zeroth lexically enclosing class of itself.* A class O is the *nth lexically enclosing class of a class* C if it is the immediately enclosing class of the *n*-1st lexically enclosing class of C. An instance *i* of a direct inner class C of a class O is associated with an instance of O, known as the *immediately enclosing instance of i.*

The immediately enclosing instance of an object, if any, is determined when the object is created. An object *o* is the *zeroth lexically enclosing instance of itself.* An object *o* is the *nth lexically enclosing instance of an instance i* if it is the immediately enclosing instance of the *n*-1st lexically enclosing instance of *i*. When an inner class refers to an instance variable that is a member of a lexically enclosing class, the variable of the corresponding lexically enclosing instance is used. A blank final field of a lexically enclosing class may not be assigned within an inner class.

An instance of an inner class *I* whose declaration occurs in a static context has no lexically enclosing instances. However, if *I* is immediately declared within a static method or static initializer then *I* does have an *enclosing block,* which is the innermost block statement lexically enclosing the declaration of *I*.

Furthermore, for every superclass *S* of *C* which is itself a direct inner class of a class *SO*, there is an instance of *SO* associated with *i*, known as the *immediately enclosing instance of i with respect to S*. The immediately enclosing instance of an object with respect to its class' direct superclass, if any, is determined when the superclass constructor is invoked via an explicit constructor invocation statement.

Any local variable, formal method parametre or exception handler parametre used but not declared in an inner class must be declared final. Any local variable, used but not declared in an inner class must be definitely assigned before the body of the inner class.

Inner classes include local, anonymous and non-static member classes. Here are some examples:

```
class Outer {
    int i = 100;
    static void classMethod() {
        final int l = 200;
        class LocalInStaticContext{
            int k = i; // compile-time error
            int m = l; // ok
        }
    }

void foo() {
```

```
    class Local { // a local class
        int j = i;
        }
    }
}
```

The declaration of class `LocalInStaticContext` occurs in a static context-within the static method `classMethod`. Instance variables of class `Outer` are not available within the body of a static method. In particular, instance variables of `Outer` are not available inside the body of `LocalInStat ic Context`. However, local variables from the surrounding method may be referred to without error (provided they are marked `final`). Inner classes whose declarations do not occur in a static context may freely refer to the instance variables of their enclosing class.

An instance variable is always defined with respect to an instance. In the case of instance variables of an enclosing class, the instance variable must be defined with respect to an enclosing instance of that class. So, for example, the class `Local` above has an enclosing instance of class `Outer`. As a further example:

```
class WithDeepNesting{
    boolean toBe;
    WithDeepNesting(boolean b) { toBe = b;}
    class Nested {
        boolean theQuestion;
        class DeeplyNested {
            DeeplyNested(){
            theQuestion = toBe || !toBe;
            }
        }
    }
}
```

Here, every instance of `WithDeepNesting. Nested. DeeplyNested` has an enclosing instance of class `WithDeepNesting.Nested` (its immediately enclosing instance) and an enclosing instance of class `WithDeepNesting` (its 2nd lexically enclosing instance).

SUPERCLASSES AND SUBCLASSES

The optional extends clause in a normal class declaration specifies the *direct superclass* of the current class.

Super:

Extends *ClassType*

The following is repeated from to make the presentation here clearer:

ClassType:

TypeDeclSpecifier TypeArguments

A class is said to be a *direct subclass* of its direct superclass. The direct superclass is the class from whose implementation the implementation of the current class is derived. The direct superclass of an enum type E is Enum<E>.

The extends clause must not appear in the definition of the class Object, because it is the primordial class and has no direct superclass.

Given a (possibly generic) class declaration for $C<F_1,...,F_n>$, $n \geq 0$, $C \neq Object$, the direct superclass of the class type $C<F_1,...,F_n>$ is the type given in the extends clause of the declaration of C if an extends clause is present, or Object otherwise.

Let $C<F_1,...,F_n>$, $n>0$, be a generic class declaration. The direct superclass of the parametreized class type $C<T_1,...,T_n>$, where T_i, $1 \leq i \leq n$, is a type, is $D<U_1\ theta ,..., U_k\ theta>$, where $D<U_1,...,U_k>$ is the direct superclass of $C<F_1,...,F_n>$, and *theta* is the substitution $[F_1 := T_1,..., F_n := T_n]$.

The *ClassType* must name an accessible class type, or a compile-time error occurs. If the specified *ClassType* names a class that is final, then a compile-time error occurs; final classes are not allowed to have subclasses.

It is a compile-time error if the *ClassType* names the class Enum or any invocation of it. If the TypeName is followed by any type arguments, it must be a correct invocation of the type declaration denoted by TypeName, and none of the type arguments may be wildcard type arguments, or a compile-time error occurs.

In the example:

```
class Point { int x, y; }
```

final class ColoredPoint extends Point { int color; } class Colored3DPoint extends ColoredPoint { int z; } // error

The relationships are as follows:

- The class Point is a direct subclass of Object.
- The class Object is the direct superclass of the class Point.
- The class ColoredPoint is a direct subclass of class Point.
- The class Point is the direct superclass of class ColoredPoint.

The declaration of class Colored3dPoint causes a compile-time error because it attempts to extend the final class ColoredPoint.

The *subclass* relationship is the transitive closure of the direct subclass relationship. A class *A* is a subclass of class *C* if either of the following is true:

- *A* is the direct subclass of *C*.
- There exists a class *B* such that *A* is a subclass of *B*, and *B* is a subclass of *C*, applying this definition recursively.

Class C is said to be a *superclass* of class *A* whenever *A* is a subclass of C.

In the example:

class Point { int x, y; }

class ColoredPoint extends Point { int color; }

final class Colored3dPoint extends ColoredPoint { int z; }

The relationships are as follows:

- The class Point is a superclass of class Colored Point.
- The class Point is a superclass of class Colored 3d Point.
- The class ColoredPoint is a subclass of class Point.
- The class ColoredPoint is a superclass of class Colored3dPoint.
- The class Colored3dPoint is a subclass of class ColoredPoint.
- The class Colored3dPoint is a subclass of class Point.

A class C *directly depends* on a type *T* if *T* is mentioned in the extends or implements clause of C either as a superclass or superinterface, or as a qualifier of a superclass or superinterface name. A class *C* depends on a reference type *T* if any of the following conditions hold:

- *C* directly depends on *T*.
- *C* directly depends on an interface *I* that depends on *T*.
- *C* directly depends on a class *D* that depends on *T* (using this definition recursively).

It is a compile-time error if a class depends on itself.

For example:

class Point extends ColoredPoint { int x, y; }

class ColoredPoint extends Point { int color; }

causes a compile-time error.

If circularly declared classes are detected at run time, as classes are loaded, then a ClassCircularityError is thrown.

SUPERINTERFACES

The optional **`implements`** clause in a class declaration lists the names of interfaces that are *direct superinterfaces* of the class being declared:

```
Interfaces:
    implements InterfaceTypeList
InterfaceTypeList:
    InterfaceType
    InterfaceTypeList , InterfaceType
```

The following is repeated from to make the presentation here clearer:

```
InterfaceType:
    TypeDeclSpecifier TypeArgumentsopt
```

Given a (possibly generic) class declaration for $C<F_1,...,F_n>$, $n \geq 0$, $C \neq Object$, the direct superinterfaces of the class type $C<F_1,...,F_n>$ are the types given in the implements clause of the declaration of *C* if an implements clause is present.

Let $C<F_1,...,F_n>$, $n>0$, be a generic class declaration. The direct superinterfaces of the parametreized class type $C<T_1,...,T_n>$, where T_i, $1 \leq i \leq n$, is a type, are all types $I<U_1$ *theta* $,..., U_k$ *theta*$>$, where $I<U_1,...,U_k>$ is a direct superinterface of $C<F_1,...,F_n>$, and *theta* is the substitution $[F_1 := T_1,..., F_n := T_n]$.

Each *InterfaceType* must name an accessible interface type, or a compile-time error occurs. If the *TypeName* is followed by any type arguments, it must be a correct invocation of the type declaration denoted by *TypeName*, and none of the type arguments may be wildcard type arguments, or a compile-time error occurs.

A compile-time error occurs if the same interface is mentioned as a direct superinterface two or more times in a single **implements** clause names.

This is true even if the interface is named in different ways; for example, the code:

```
class Redundant implements java. lang. Cloneable,
Cloneable {
    int x;
}
```

results in a compile-time error because the names java.lang.**Cloneable** and **Cloneable** refer to the same interface.

An interface type *I* is a *superinterface* of class type C if any of the following is true:

- *I* is a direct superinterface of C.
- *C* has some direct superinterface *J* for which *I* is a superinterface, using the definition of "superinterface of an interface" given in.
- *I* is a superinterface of the direct superclass of C.

A class is said to *implement* all its superinterfaces.

In the example:

```
public interface Colorable {
    void setColor(int color);
    int getColor();
}
public enum Finish {MATTE, GLOSSY}
public interface Paintable extends Colorable {
    void setFinish(Finish finish);
    Finish getFinish();
}
class Point { int x, y; }
class ColoredPoint extends Point implements
```

```
    Colorable {
    int color;
    public void setColor(int color) { this.color
    = color; }
    public int getColor() { return color; }
}
class PaintedPoint extends ColoredPoint
    implements Paintable
{
    Finish finish;
    public void setFinish(Finish finish) {
    this.finish = finish;
    }
    public Finish getFinish() { return finish;
    }
}
```

the relationships are as follows:

- The interface Paintable is a superinterface of class PaintedPoint.
- The interface Colorable is a superinterface of class ColoredPoint and of class PaintedPoint.
- The interface Paintable is a subinterface of the interface Colorable, and Colorable is a superinterface of Paintable.

A class can have a superinterface in more than one way. In this example, the class `PaintedPoint` has `Colorable` as a superinterface both because it is a superinterface of `ColoredPoint` and because it is a superinterface of `Paintable`. Unless the class being declared is `abstract`, the declarations of all the method members of each direct superinterface must be implemented either by a declaration in this class or by an existing method declaration inherited from the direct superclass, because a class that is not `abstract` is not permitted to have `abstract` methods.

Thus, the example:

```
interface Colorable {
    void setColor(int color);
    int getColor();
```

```
}
class Point { int x, y; };
class ColoredPoint extends Point implements
    Colorable {
    int color;
}
```

causes a compile-time error, because **ColoredPoint** is not an **abstract** class but it fails to provide an implementation of methods **setColor** and **getColor** of the interface **Colorable**.

It is permitted for a single method declaration in a class to implement methods of more than one superinterface. For example, in the code:

```
    interface Fish { int getNumberOfScales(); }
    interface Piano { int getNumberOfScales();
}
    class Tuna implements Fish, Piano {
        // You can tune a piano, but can you
tuna fish?
        int getNumberOfScales() { return 91; }
    }
```

the method **getNumberOfScales** in class **Tuna** has a name, signature, and return type that matches the method declared in interface **Fish** and also matches the method declared in interface **Piano**; it is considered to implement both.

On the other hand, in a situation such as this:

```
interface Fish { int getNumberOfScales(); }
interface StringBass { double
    getNumberOfScales(); }
class Bass implements Fish, StringBass {
    // This declaration cannot be correct, no
    matter what type is used.
    public ??? getNumberOfScales() { return 91;
    }
}
```

It is impossible to declare a method named **getNumberOfScales** whose signature and return type are compatible with those of both the methods declared in interface

Fish and in interface **StringBass**, because a class cannot have multiple methods with the same signature and different primitive return types. Therefore, it is impossible for a single class to implement both interface **Fish** and interface **StringBass**. A class may not at the same time be a subtype of two interface types which are different invocations of the same generic interface, or an invocation of a generic interface and a raw type naming that same generic interface.

Here is an example of an illegal multiple inheritance of an interface:

```
class B implements I<Integer>
class C extends B implements I<String>
```

This requirement was introduced in order to support translation by type erasure.

CLASS BODY AND MEMBER DECLARATIONS

A *class body* may contain declarations of members of the class, that is, fields, classes, interfaces and methods. A class body may also contain instance initializers, static initializers, and declarations of constructors for the class.

```
ClassBody:
    { ClassBodyDeclarationsopt }
ClassBodyDeclarations:
    ClassBodyDeclaration
    ClassBodyDeclarations ClassBodyDeclaration
ClassBodyDeclaration:
    ClassMemberDeclaration
    InstanceInitializer
    StaticInitializer
    ConstructorDeclaration
ClassMemberDeclaration:
    FieldDeclaration
    MethodDeclaration
    ClassDeclaration
    InterfaceDeclaration
    ;
```

The scope of a declaration of a member *m* declared in or inherited by a class type *C* is the entire body of *C*, including any nested type declarations. If C itself is a nested class, there may be definitions of the same kind (variable, method, or type) and name as *m* in enclosing scopes. (The scopes may be blocks, classes, or packages.) In all such cases, the member *m* declared or inherited in C shadows the other definitions of the same kind and name.

CLASS MEMBERS

The members of a class type are all of the following:

- Members inherited from its direct superclass, except in class Object, which has no direct superclass
- Members inherited from any direct superinterfaces
- Members declared in the body of the class

Members of a class that are declared **`private`** are not inherited by subclasses of that class. Only members of a class that are declared **`protected`** or **`public`** are inherited by subclasses declared in a package other than the one in which the class is declared.

We use the phrase *the type of a member* to denote:

- For a field, its type.
- For a method, an ordered 3-tuple consisting of:
  - Argument types: a list of the types of the arguments to the method member.
  - Return type: the return type of the method member and the
  - Throws clause: exception types declared in the throws clause of the method member.

Constructors, static initializers, and instance initializers are not members and therefore are not inherited.

The example:

```
class Point {
   int x, y;
   private Point() { reset(); }
   Point(int x, int y) { this.x = x; this.y =
   y; }
   private void reset() { this.x = 0; this.y =
   0; }
}
```

```
class ColoredPoint extends Point {
    int color;
    void clear() { reset(); }
          // error
}
class Test {
    public static void main(String[] args) {
          ColoredPoint c = new ColoredPoint(0,
    0);   // error
          c.reset();
    // error
    }
}
```

Causes four compile-time errors:

- An error occurs because ColoredPoint has no constructor declared with two integer parametres, as requested by the use in main. This illustrates the fact that ColoredPoint does not inherit the constructors of its superclass Point.
- Another error occurs because ColoredPoint declares no constructors, and therefore a default constructor for it is automatically created, and this default constructor is equivalent to:
- ColoredPoint() { super(); }

which invokes the constructor, with no arguments, for the direct superclass of the class `ColoredPoint`. The error is that the constructor for `Point` that takes no arguments is `private`, and therefore is not accessible outside the class `Point`, even through a superclass constructor invocation.

Two more errors occur because the method `reset` of class `Point` is `private`, and therefore is not inherited by class `ColoredPoint`. The method invocations in method `clear` of class `ColoredPoint` and in method `main` of class `Test` are therefore not correct.

EXAMPLES OF INHERITANCE

This section illustrates inheritance of class members through several examples.

Example: Inheritance with Default Access

Consider the example where the **points** package declares two compilation units:

```
package points;
public class Point {
    int x, y;
    public void move(int dx, int dy) { x += dx;
    y += dy; }
}
```

and:

```
package points;
public class Point3d extends Point {
    int z;
    public void move(int dx, int dy, int dz) {
        x += dx; y += dy; z += dz;
    }
}
```

and a third compilation unit, in another package, is:

```
import points.Point3d;
class Point4d extends Point3d {
    int w;
    public void move(int dx, int dy, int dz,
    int dw) {
        x += dx; y += dy; z += dz; w += dw; /
    / compile-time errors
    }
}
```

Here both classes in the **points** package compile. The class **Point3d** inherits the fields **x** and **y** of class **Point**, because it is in the same package as **Point**. The class **Point4d**, which is in a different package, does not inherit the fields **x** and **y** of class **Point** or the field **z** of class **Point3d**, and so fails to compile.

A better way to write the third compilation unit would be:

```
import points.Point3d;
class Point4d extends Point3d {
    int w;
```

```
    public void move(int dx, int dy, int dz,
    int dw) {
    super.move(dx, dy, dz); w += dw;
    }
}
```

using the **move** method of the superclass **Point3d** to process **dx**, **dy**, and **dz**. If **Point4d** is written in this way it will compile without errors.

INHERITANCE WITH PUBLIC AND PROTECTED

Given the class **Point**:

```
package points;
public class Point {
    public int x, y;
    protected int useCount = 0;
    static protected int totalUseCount = 0;
    public void move(int dx, int dy) {
        x += dx; y += dy; useCount++;
    totalUseCount++;
    }
}
```

the **public** and **protected** fields **x**, **y**, **useCount** and **totalUseCount** are inherited in all subclasses of **Point**.

Therefore, this test program, in another package, can be compiled successfully:

```
class Test extends points.Point {
    public void moveBack(int dx, int dy) {
        x -= dx; y -= dy; useCount++;
    totalUseCount++;
    }
}
```

INHERITANCE WITH PRIVATE

In the example:

```
class Point {
    int x, y;
    void move(int dx, int dy) {
        x += dx; y += dy; totalMoves++;
```

```
    }
    private static int totalMoves;
    void printMoves() {
System.out.println(totalMoves); }
}
class Point3d extends Point {
    int z;
    void move(int dx, int dy, int dz) {
        super.move(dx, dy); z += dz;
    totalMoves++;
    }
}
```

the class variable **totalMoves** can be used only within the class **Point**; it is not inherited by the subclass **Point3d**. A compile-time error occurs because method **move** of class **Point3d** tries to increment **totalMoves**.

ACCESSING MEMBERS OF INACCESSIBLE CLASSES

Even though a class might not be declared **public**, instances of the class might be available at run time to code outside the package in which it is declared by means a **public** superclass or superinterface. An instance of the class can be assigned to a variable of such a **public** type. An invocation of a **public** method of the object referred to by such a variable may invoke a method of the class if it implements or overrides a method of the **public** superclass or superinterface. (In this situation, the method is necessarily declared **public**, even though it is declared in a class that is not **public**.)

Consider the compilation unit:

```
package points;
public class Point {
    public int x, y;
    public void move(int dx, int dy) {
        x += dx; y += dy;
    }
}
```

and another compilation unit of another package:

```
package morePoints;
class Point3d extends points.Point {
    public int z;
    public void move(int dx, int dy, int dz) {
        super.move(dx, dy); z += dz;
    }
    public void move(int dx, int dy) {
        move(dx, dy, 0);
    }
}
public class OnePoint {
    public static points.Point getOne() {
        return new Point3d();
    }
}
```

An invocation `morePoints.OnePoint.getOne()` in yet a third package would return a `Point3d` that can be used as a `Point`, even though the type `Point3d` is not available outside the package `morePoints`. The two argument version of method `move` could then be invoked for that object, which is permissible because method `move` of `Point3d` is `public` (as it must be, for any method that overrides a `public` method must itself be `public`, precisely so that situations such as this will work out correctly). The fields `x` and `y` of that object could also be accessed from such a third package.

While the field `z` of class `Point3d` is `public`, it is not possible to access this field from code outside the package `morePoints`, given only a reference to an instance of class `Point3d` in a variable `p` of type `Point`. This is because the expression `p.z` is not correct, as `p` has type `Point` and class `Point` has no field named `z`; also, the expression `((Point3d)p).z` is not correct, because the class type `Point3d` cannot be referred to outside package `morePoints`.

The declaration of the field `z` as `public` is not useless, however. If there were to be, in package `morePoints`, a `public` subclass `Point4d` of the class `Point3d`:

```
package morePoints;
public class Point4d extends Point3d {
```

```
    public int w;
    public void move(int dx, int dy, int dz,
    int dw) {
            super.move(dx, dy, dz); w += dw;
    }
}
```

then class **Point4d** would inherit the field **z**, which, being **public**, could then be accessed by code in packages other than **morePoints**, through variables and expressions of the **public** type **Point4d**.

FIELD DECLARATIONS

The variables of a class type are introduced by *field declarations*:

```
FieldDeclaration:
    FieldModifiersopt Type VariableDeclarators
    ;
VariableDeclarators:
    VariableDeclarator
    VariableDeclarators , VariableDeclarator
VariableDeclarator:
    VariableDeclaratorId
    VariableDeclaratorId = VariableInitializer
VariableDeclaratorId:
    Identifier
    VariableDeclaratorId [ ]
VariableInitializer:
    Expression
        ArrayInitializer
```

It is a compile-time error for the body of a class declaration to declare two fields with the same name. Methods, types, and fields may have the same name, since they are used in different contexts and are disambiguated by different lookup procedures.

If the class declares a field with a certain name, then the declaration of that field is said to *hide* any and all accessible declarations of fields with the same name in superclasses, and superinterfaces of the class.

The field declaration also shadows declarations of any accessible fields in enclosing classes or interfaces, and any local variables, formal method parametres, and exception handler parametres with the same name in any enclosing blocks.

If a field declaration hides the declaration of another field, the two fields need not have the same type. A class inherits from its direct superclass and direct superinterfaces all the non-private fields of the superclass and superinterfaces that are both accessible to code in the class and not hidden by a declaration in the class.

Note that a private field of a superclass might be accessible to a subclass (for example, if both classes are members of the same class). Nevertheless, a private field is never inherited by a subclass.

It is possible for a class to inherit more than one field with the same name.Such a situation does not in itself cause a compile-time error. However, any attempt within the body of the class to refer to any such field by its simple name will result in a compile-time error, because such a reference is ambiguous. There might be several paths by which the same field declaration might be inherited from an interface.

In such a situation, the field is considered to be inherited only once, and it may be referred to by its simple name without ambiguity. A hidden field can be accessed by using a qualified name (if it is **`static`**) or by using a field access expression that contains the keyword **`super`** or a cast to a superclass type. A value stored in a field of type **`float`** is always an element of the float value set; similarly, a value stored in a field of type **`double`** is always an element of the double value set.

It is not permitted for a field of type **`float`** to contain an element of the float-extended-exponent value set that is not also an element of the float value set, nor for a field of type **`double`** to contain an element of the double-extended-exponent value set that is not also an element of the double value set.

FIELD MODIFIERS

```
FieldModifiers:
    FieldModifier
```

```
    FieldModifiers FieldModifier
FieldModifier: one of
    Annotation public protected private
    static final transient volatile
```

A compile-time error occurs if the same modifier appears more than once in a field declaration, or if a field declaration has more than one of the access modifiers **public**, **protected**, and **private**.

If an annotation *a* on a field declaration corresponds to an annotation type *T*, and *T* has a (meta-)annotation *m* that corresponds to **annotation.Target**, then *m* must have an element whose value is **annotation.ElementType.FIELD**, or a compile-time error occurs. Annotation modifiers are described later.

If two or more (distinct) field modifiers appear in a field declaration, it is customary, though not required, that they appear in the order consistent with that shown above in the production for *FieldModifier*.

STATIC FIELDS

If a field is declared **static**, there exists exactly one incarnation of the field, no matter how many instances (possibly zero) of the class may eventually be created. A **static** field, sometimes called a *class variable*, is incarnated when the class is initialized.

A field that is not declared **static** (sometimes called a non-**static** field) is called an *instance variable*. Whenever a new instance of a class is created, a new variable associated with that instance is created for every instance variable declared in that class or any of its superclasses. The example program:

```
class Point {
    int x, y, useCount;
    Point(int x, int y) { this.x = x; this.y =
    y; }
    final static Point origin = new Point(0,
    0);
}
class Test {
```

```
    public static void main(String[] args) {
          Point p = new Point(1,1);
          Point q = new Point(2,2);
          p.x  =  3;  p.y  =  3;  p.useCount++;
    p.origin.useCount++;
          System.out.println("(" + q.x + "," +
    q.y + ")");
          System.out.println(q.useCount);
          System.out.println(q.origin  ==
    Point.origin);

    System.out.println(q.origin.useCount);
    }
}
prints:
(2,2)
0
true
1
```

showing that changing the fields **x**, **y**, and **useCount** of **p** does not affect the fields of **q**, because these fields are instance variables in distinct objects. In this example, the class variable **origin** of the class **Point** is referenced both using the class name as a qualifier, in **Point.origin**, and using variables of the class type in field access expressions, as in **p.origin** and **q.origin**.

These two ways of accessing the **origin** class variable access the same object, evidenced by the fact that the value of the reference equality expression:

q.origin==Point.origin

is **true**. Further evidence is that the incrementation:

p.origin.useCount++;

causes the value of **q.origin.useCount** to be **1**; this is so because **p.origin** and **q.origin** refer to the same variable.

FINAL FIELDS

A field can be declared **final**. Both class and instance variables (**static** and non-**static** fields) may be declared `final`. It is a compile-time error if a blank final class variable is not definitely assigned by a static initializer of the class in which it is declared.

A blank final instance variable must be definitely assigned at the end of every constructor of the class in which it is declared; otherwise a compile-time error occurs.

TRANSIENT FIELDS

Variables may be marked `transient` to indicate that they are not part of the persistent state of an object.

If an instance of the class `Point`:

```
class Point {
    int x, y;
    transient float rho, theta;
}
```

were saved to persistent storage by a system service, then only the fields `x` and `y` would be saved. This specification does not specify details of such services; see the specification of `java.io.Serializable` for an example of such a service.

VOLATILE FIELDS

The Java programming language allows threads to access shared variables. As a rule, to ensure that shared variables are consistently and reliably updated, a thread should ensure that it has exclusive use of such variables by obtaining a lock that, conventionally, enforces mutual exclusion for those shared variables.

The Java programming language provides a second mechanism, volatile fields, that is more convenient than locking for some purposes.

A field may be declared `volatile`, in which case the Java memory model ensures that all threads see a consistent value for the variable.

If, in the following example, one thread repeatedly calls the method `one` (but no more than `Integer.MAX_VALUE` times in all), and another thread repeatedly calls the method `two`:

```
class Test {
    static int i = 0, j = 0;
```

```
    static void one() { i++; j++; }
    static void two() {
    System.out.println("i=" + i + " j=" + j);
    }
}
```

then method **two** could occasionally print a value for `j` that is greater than the value of `i`, because the example includes no synchronization and, under the rules explained in, the shared values of `i` and `j` might be updated out of order. One way to prevent this out-or-order behaviour would be to declare methods **one** and **two** to be **synchronized**:

```
class Test {
    static int i = 0, j = 0;
    static synchronized void one() { i++; j++;
    }
    static synchronized void two() {
        System.out.println("i=" + i + " j=" +
    j);
    }
}
```

This prevents method **one** and method **two** from being executed concurrently, and furthermore guarantees that the shared values of `i` and `j` are both updated before method **one** returns. Therefore method **two** never observes a value for `j` greater than that for `i`; indeed, it always observes the same value for `i` and `j`.

Another approach would be to declare `i` and `j` to be `volatile`:

```
class Test {
    static volatile int i = 0, j = 0;
    static void one() { i++; j++; }
    static void two() {
        System.out.println("i=" + i + " j=" +
    j);
    }
}
```

This allows method **one** and method **two** to be executed concurrently, but guarantees that accesses to the shared values for `i` and `j` occur exactly as many times, and in exactly the same order, as they appear to occur during execution of the program text by each thread.

Therefore, the shared value for `j` is never greater than that for `i`, because each update to `i` must be reflected in the shared value for `i` before the update to `j` occurs. It is possible, however, that any given invocation of method `two` might observe a value for `j` that is much greater than the value observed for `i`, because method `one` might be executed many times between the moment when method `two` fetches the value of `i` and the moment when method `two` fetches the value of `j`. A compile-time error occurs if a **`final`** variable is also declared **`volatile`**.

INITIALIZATION OF FIELDS

If a field declarator contains a *variable initializer*, then it has the semantics of an assignment to the declared variable, and:

- If the declarator is for a class variable (that is, a static field), then the variable initializer is evaluated and the assignment performed exactly once, when the class is initialized.
- If the declarator is for an instance variable (that is, a field that is not static), then the variable initializer is evaluated and the assignment performed each time an instance of the class is created.

The example:

```
class Point {
    int x = 1, y = 5;
}
class Test {
    public static void main(String[] args) {
         Point p = new Point();
         System.out.println(p.x + ", " + p.y);
    }
}
```

produces the output:

```
1, 5
```

because the assignments to `x` and `y` occur whenever a new `Point` is created.

Variable initializers are also used in local variable declaration statements, where the initializer is evaluated and the assignment performed each time the local variable declaration statement is executed.

It is a compile-time error if the evaluation of a variable initializer for a `static` field of a named class (or of an interface) can complete abruptly with a checked exception.

It is compile-time error if an instance variable initializer of a named class can throw a checked exception unless that exception or one of its supertypes is explicitly declared in the throws clause of each constructor of its class and the class has at least one explicitly declared constructor. An instance variable initializer in an anonymous class can throw any exceptions.

INITIALIZERS FOR CLASS VARIABLES

If a reference by simple name to any instance variable occurs in an initialization expression for a class variable, then a compile-time error occurs.

If the keyword `this` or the keyword `super` occurs in an initialization expression for a class variable, then a compile-time error occurs.

One subtlety here is that, at run time, `static` variables that are `final` and that are initialized with compile-time constant values are initialized first. This also applies to such fields in interfaces. These variables are "constants" that will never be observed to have their default initial values, even by devious programs.

Use of class variables whose declarations appear textually after the use is sometimes restricted, even though these class variables are in scope.The precise rules governing forward reference to class variables.

INITIALIZERS FOR INSTANCE VARIABLES

Initialization expressions for instance variables may use the simple name of any `static` variable declared in or inherited by the class, even one whose declaration occurs textually later.

`Thus the example:`

```
class Test {
    float f = j;
    static int j = 1;
}
```

compiles without error; it initializes `j` to `1` when class `Test` is initialized, and initializes `f` to the current value of `j` every time an instance of class `Test` is created.

Initialization expressions for instance variables are permitted to refer to the current object **`this`** and to use the keyword **`super`**. Use of instance variables whose declarations appear textually after the use is sometimes restricted, even though these instance variables are in scope. The precise rules governing forward reference to instance variables.

RESTRICTIONS ON THE USE OF FIELDS DURING INITIALIZATION

The declaration of a member needs to appear textually before it is used only if the member is an instance (respectively **`static`**) field of a class or interface C and all of the following conditions hold:

- The usage occurs in an instance (respectively static) variable initializer of C or in an instance (respectively static) initializer of C.
- The usage is not on the left hand side of an assignment.
- The usage is via a simple name.
- C is the innermost class or interface enclosing the usage.

A compile-time error occurs if any of the four requirements above are not met.

This means that a compile-time error results from the test program:

```
class Test {
    int i = j; // compile-time error:
incorrect forward reference
    int j = 1;
}
```

whereas the following example compiles without

```
error:
class Test {
      Test() { k = 2; }
      int j = 1;
      int i = j;
      int k;
}
```

even though the constructor for **Test** refers to the field **k** that is declared three lines later. These restrictions are designed to catch, at compile time, circular or otherwise malformed initializations.

Thus, both:

```
class Z {
    static int i = j + 2;
    static int j = 4;
}
```

and:

```
class Z {
    static { i = j + 2; }
    static int i, j;
    static { j = 4; }
}
```

result in compile-time errors. Accesses by methods are not checked in this way, so:

```
class Z {
    static int peek() { return j; }
    static int i = peek();
    static int j = 1;
}
class Test {
    public static void main(String[] args) {
          System.out.println(Z.i);
    }
}
```

produces the output:

```
0
```

because the variable initializer for **i** uses the class method **peek** to access the value of the variable **j** before **j** has been initialized by its variable initializer, at which point it still has its default value.

A more elaborate example is:

```
class UseBeforeDeclaration {
    static {
        x = 100; // ok - assignment
        int y = x + 1; // error - read before
    declaration
        int v = x = 3; // ok - x at left hand
    side of assignment
        int z = UseBeforeDeclaration.x * 2;
    // ok - not accessed via simple name
        Object o = new Object(){
            void foo(){x++;} // ok - occurs
    in a different class
            {x++;} // ok - occurs in a
    different class
        };
   }
    {
        j = 200; // ok - assignment
        j = j + 1; // error - right hand side
    reads before declaration
        int k = j = j + 1;
        int n = j = 300; // ok - j at left
    hand side of assignment
        int h = j++; // error - read before
    declaration
        int l = this.j * 3; // ok - not accessed
    via simple name
        Object o = new Object(){
            void foo(){j++;} // ok - occurs
    in a different class
            { j = j + 1;} // ok - occurs in
    a different class
        };
    }
    int w = x = 3; // ok - x at left hand side
```

```
    of assignment
    int p = x; // ok - instance initializers
    may access static fields
    static int u = (new Object(){int
    bar(){return x;}}).bar();
    // ok - occurs in a different class
    static int x;
    int m = j = 4; // ok - j at left hand side
    of assignment
    int o = (new Object(){int bar(){return
    j;}}).bar();
    // ok - occurs in a different class
    int j;
}
```

EXAMPLES OF FIELD DECLARATIONS

The following examples illustrate some (possibly subtle) points about field declarations.

HIDING OF CLASS VARIABLES

The example:

```
class Point {
    static int x = 2;
}
class Test extends Point {
    static double x = 4.7;
    public static void main(String[] args) {
        new Test().printX();
    }
    void printX() {
        System.out.println(x + " " + super.x);
    }
}
```

Produces the output:

```
4.7 2
```

because the declaration of **x** in class **Test** hides the definition of **x** in class **Point**, so class **Test** does not inherit the field **x** from its superclass **Point**. Within the declaration of class **Test**, the simple name **x** refers to the field declared within class **Test**. Code in class **Test** may refer to the field **x** of class **Point** as **super.x** (or, because **x** is **static**, as **Point.x**). If the declaration of **Test.x** is deleted:

```
class Point {
    static int x = 2;
}
class Test extends Point {
    public static void main(String[] args) {
        new Test().printX();
    }
    void printX() {
        System.out.println(x + " " + super.x);
    }
}
```

then the field **x** of class **Point** is no longer hidden within class **Test**; instead, the simple name **x** now refers to the field **Point.x**. Code in class **Test** may still refer to that same field as **super.x**. Therefore, the output from this variant program is:

```
2 2
```

HIDING OF INSTANCE VARIABLES

This example is similar to that in the previous section, but uses instance variables rather than static variables. The code:

```
class Point {
    int x = 2;
}
class Test extends Point {
    double x = 4.7;
    void printBoth() {
        System.out.println(x + " " + super.x);
    }
    public static void main(String[] args) {
        Test sample = new Test();
        sample.printBoth();
        System.out.println(sample.x + " " +
    ((Point)sample).x);
```

```
    }
}
```

produces the output:

```
4.7 2
4.7 2
```

because the declaration of **x** in class **Test** hides the definition of **x** in class **Point**, so class **Test** does not inherit the field **x** from its superclass **Point**. It must be noted, however, that while the field **x** of class **Point** is not *inherited* by class **Test**, it is nevertheless *implemented* by instances of class **Test**. In other words, every instance of class **Test** contains two fields, one of type **int** and one of type **double**. Both fields bear the name **x**, but within the declaration of class **Test**, the simple name **x** always refers to the field declared within class **Test**. Code in instance methods of class **Test** may refer to the instance variable **x** of class **Point** as **super.x**.

Code that uses a field access expression to access field **x** will access the field named **x** in the class indicated by the type of reference expression. Thus, the expression **sample.x** accesses a **double** value, the instance variable declared in class **Test**, because the type of the variable sample is **Test**, but the expression **((Point)sample).x** accesses an **int** value, the instance variable declared in class **Point**, because of the cast to type **Point**.

If the declaration of **x** is deleted from class **Test**, as in the program:

```
class Point {
    static int x = 2;
}
class Test extends Point {
    void printBoth() {
        System.out.println(x + " " + super.x);
    }
    public static void main(String[] args) {
        Test sample = new Test();
        sample.printBoth();
        System.out.println(sample.x + " " +
        ((Point)sample).x);
```

```
    }
}
```

then the field **x** of class **Point** is no longer hidden within class **Test**. Within instance methods in the declaration of class **Test**, the simple name **x** now refers to the field declared within class **Point**.

Code in class **Test** may still refer to that same field as **super.x**. The expression **sample.x** still refers to the field **x** within type **Test**, but that field is now an inherited field, and so refers to the field **x** declared in class **Point**. The output from this variant program is:

```
2 2
2 2
```

MULTIPLY INHERITED FIELDS

A class may inherit two or more fields with the same name, either from two interfaces or from its superclass and an interface.

A compile-time error occurs on any attempt to refer to any ambiguously inherited field by its simple name. A qualified name or a field access expression that contains the keyword **super** may be used to access such fields unambiguously. In the example:

```
interface Frob { float v = 2.0f; }
class SuperTest { int v = 3; }
class Test extends SuperTest implements Frob {
    public static void main(String[] args) {
        new Test().printV();
    }
    void printV() { System.out.println(v); }
}
```

the class **Test** inherits two fields named **v**, one from its superclass **SuperTest** and one from its superinterface **Frob**. This in itself is permitted, but a compile-time error occurs because of the use of the simple name **v** in method **printV**: it cannot be determined which **v** is intended.

The following variation uses the field access expression **super.v** to refer to the field named **v** declared in class

SuperTest and uses the qualified name **Frob.v** to refer to the field named **v** declared in interface **Frob**:

```
interface Frob { float v = 2.0f; }
class SuperTest { int v = 3; }
class Test extends SuperTest implements Frob {
    public static void main(String[] args) {
         new Test().printV();
    }
    void printV() {
    System.out.println((super.v + Frob.v)/2);
    }
}
It compiles and prints:
2.5
```

Even if two distinct inherited fields have the same type, the same value, and are both **final**, any reference to either field by simple name is considered ambiguous and results in a compile-time error. In the example:

```
interface Color { int RED=0, GREEN=1, BLUE=2;
    }
interface TrafficLight { int RED=0, YELLOW=1,
    GREEN=2; }
class Test implements Color, TrafficLight {
    public static void main(String[] args) {
         System.out.println(GREEN); // compile-
    time error
         System.out.println(RED); // compile-
    time error
    }
}
```

It is not astonishing that the reference to **GREEN** should be considered ambiguous, because class **Test** inherits two different declarations for **GREEN** with different values. The point of this example is that the reference to **RED** is also considered ambiguous, because two distinct declarations are inherited. The fact that the two fields named **RED** happen to have the same type and the same unchanging value does not affect this judgment.

RE-INHERITANCE OF FIELDS

If the same field declaration is inherited from an interface by multiple paths, the field is considered to be inherited only once. It may be referred to by its simple name without ambiguity. For example, in the code:

```
public interface Colorable {
    int RED = 0xff0000, GREEN = 0x00ff00, BLUE
    = 0x0000ff;
}
public interface Paintable extends Colorable {
    int MATTE = 0, GLOSSY = 1;
}
class Point { int x, y; }
class ColoredPoint extends Point implements
    Colorable {
    ...
}
class PaintedPoint extends ColoredPoint
    implements Paintable
{
    ...        RED    ...
}
```

the fields RED, GREEN, and BLUE are inherited by the class PaintedPoint both through its direct superclass ColoredPoint and through its direct superinterface Paintable. The simple names RED, GREEN, and BLUE may nevertheless be used without ambiguity within the class PaintedPoint to refer to the fields declared in interface Colorable.

METHOD DECLARATIONS

A *method* declares executable code that can be invoked, passing a fixed number of values as arguments.

```
MethodDeclaration:
    MethodHeader MethodBody
MethodHeader:
    MethodModifiersopt TypeParametresopt
    ResultType MethodDeclarator
Throwsopt
```

```
ResultType:
    Type
    void
MethodDeclarator:
    Identifier ( FormalParametreListopt )
```

A method declaration either specifies the type of value that the method returns or uses the keyword **void** to indicate that the method does not return a value. The *Identifier* in a *MethodDeclarator* may be used in a name to refer to the method. A class can declare a method with the same name as the class or a field, member class or member interface of the class, but this is discouraged as a matter of syle.

For compatibility with older versions of the Java platform, a declaration form for a method that returns an array is allowed to place (some or all of) the empty bracket pairs that form the declaration of the array type after the parametre list. This is supported by the obsolescent production:

```
MethodDeclarator:
    MethodDeclarator [ ]
```

but should not be used in new code.

It is a compile-time error for the body of a class to declare as members two methods with override-equivalent signatures (name, number of parametres, and types of any parametres). Methods and fields may have the same name, since they are used in different contexts and are disambiguated by different lookup procedures.

FORMAL PARAMETRES

The *formal parametres* of a method or constructor, if any, are specified by a list of comma-separated parametre specifiers. Each parametre specifier consists of a type (optionally preceded by the **final** modifier and/or one or more annotations) and an identifier (optionally followed by brackets) that specifies the name of the parametre. The last formal parametre in a list is special; it may be a *variable arity parametre,* indicated by an elipsis following the type:

```
FormalParametreList:
    LastFormalParametre
```

```
    FormalParametres , LastFormalParametre
FormalParametres:
    FormalParametre
    FormalParametres , FormalParametre
FormalParametre:
    VariableModifiers Type VariableDeclaratorId
VariableModifiers:
    VariableModifier
    VariableModifiers VariableModifier
VariableModifier: one of
    final Annotation
LastFormalParametre:
    VariableModifiers Type...opt
    VariableDeclaratorId
    FormalParametre
```

The following is repeated from to make the presentation here clearer:

```
VariableDeclaratorId:
    Identifier
    VariableDeclaratorId [ ]
```

If a method or constructor has no parametres, only an empty pair of parentheses appears in the declaration of the method or constructor. If two formal parametres of the same method or constructor are declared to have the same name (that is, their declarations mention the same *Identifier*), then a compile-time error occurs.

If an annotation *a* on a formal parametre corresponds to an annotation type *T*, and *T* has a (meta-)annotation *m* that corresponds to `annotation.Target`, then *m* must have an element whose value is `annotation.ElementType.PARAMETRE`, or a compile-time error occurs.

It is a compile-time error if a method or constructor parametre that is declared final is assigned to within the body of the method or constructor. When the method or constructor is invoked, the values of the actual argument expressions initialize newly created parametre variables, each of the declared *Type*, before execution of the body of the method or constructor.

The *Identifier* that appears in the *DeclaratorId* may be used as a simple name in the body of the method or constructor to refer to the formal parametre. If the last formal parametre is a variable arity parametre of type *T*, it is considered to define a formal parametre of type *T[]*. The method is then a *variable arity method*.

Otherwise, it is a *fixed arity method*. Invocations of a variable arity method may contain more actual argument expressions than formal parametres. All the actual argument expressions that do not correspond to the formal parametres preceding the variable arity parametre will be evaluated and the results stored into an array that will be passed to the method invocation.

The scope of a parametre of a method or constructor is the entire body of the method or constructor. These parametre names may not be redeclared as local variables of the method, or as exception parametres of catch clauses in a try statement of the method or constructor. However, a parametre of a method or constructor may be shadowed anywhere inside a class declaration nested within that method or constructor. Such a nested class declaration could declare either a local class or an anonymous class.

Formal parametres are referred to only using simple names, never by using qualified names. A method or constructor parametre of type `float` always contains an element of the float value set; similarly, a method or constructor parametre of type `double` always contains an element of the double value set. It is not permitted for a method or constructor parametre of type `float` to contain an element of the float-extended-exponent value set that is not also an element of the float value set, nor for a method parametre of type `double` to contain an element of the double-extended-exponent value set that is not also an element of the double value set.

Where an actual argument expression corresponding to a parametre variable is not FP-strict, evaluation of that actual argument expression is permitted to use intermediate values drawn from the appropriate extended-exponent value sets. Prior to being stored in the parametre variable the result of such an expression is mapped to the nearest value in the corresponding standard value set by method invocation conversion.

Method Signature

It is a compile-time error to declare two methods with override-equivalent signatures (defined below) in a class. Two methods have the *same signature* if they have the same name and argument types. Two method or constructor declarations *M* and *N* have the *same argument types* if all of the following conditions hold:

- They have the same number of formal parametres (possibly zero)
- They have the same number of type parametres (possibly zero)
- Let $<A_1,...,A_n>$ be the formal type parametres of *M* and let $<B_1,...,B_n>$ be the formal type parametres of *N*. After renaming each occurrence of a B_i in *N*'s type to A_i the bounds of corresponding type variables and the argument types of *M* and *N* are the same.

The signature of a method *m1* is a *subsignature* of the signature of a method *m2* if either

- *m2* has the same signature as *m1*, or
- The signature of *m1* is the same as the erasure of the signature of *m2*.

Discussion : The notion of subsignature defined here is designed to express a relationship between two methods whose signatures are not identical, but in which one may override the other.

Specifically, it allows a method whose signature does not use generic types to override any generified version of that method. This is important so that library designers may freely generify methods independently of clients that define subclasses or subinterfaces of the library.

Consider the example:

```
class CollectionConverter {
   List toList(Collection c) {...}
}
```

```
class Overrider extends CollectionConverter{
    List toList(Collection c) {...}
}
```

Now, assume this code was written before the introduction of genericity, and now the author of class **CollectionConverter** decides to generify the code, thus:

```
class CollectionConverter {
    <T> List<T> toList(Collection<T> c) {...}
}
```

Without special dispensation, **Overrider.toList()** would no longer override **CollectionConverter.toList()**. Instead, the code would be illegal. This would significantly inhibit the use of genericity, since library writers would hesitate to migrate existing code. Two method signatures *m1* and *m2* are *override-equivalent* iff either *m1* is a subsignature of *m2* or *m2* is a subsignature of *m1*.

The example:

```
class Point implements Move {
    int x, y;
    abstract void move(int dx, int dy);
    void move(int dx, int dy) { x += dx; y +=
    dy; }
}
```

causes a compile-time error because it declares two **move** methods with the same (and hence, override-equivalent) signature. This is an error even though one of the declarations is **abstract**.

METHOD MODIFIERS

```
MethodModifiers:
    MethodModifier
    MethodModifiers MethodModifier
MethodModifier: one of
    Annotation public protected private abstract
    static
        final synchronized native strictfp
```

A compile-time error occurs if the same modifier appears more than once in a method declaration, or if a method declaration has more than one of the access modifiers **public**, **protected**, and **private**. A compile-time error occurs if a method declaration that contains the keyword **abstract** also contains any one of the keywords **private**, **static**, **final**, **native**, **strictfp**, or **synchronized**. A compile-time error occurs if a method declaration that contains the keyword **native** also contains **strictfp**.

If an annotation *a* on a method declaration corresponds to an annotation type *T*, and *T* has a (meta-)annotation *m* that corresponds to **annotation.Target**, then *m* must have an element whose value is **annotation.ElementType.METHOD**, or a compile-time error occurs. If two or more method modifiers appear in a method declaration, it is customary, though not required, that they appear in the order consistent with that shown above in the production for *MethodModifier*.

Abstract Methods

An **abstract** method declaration introduces the method as a member, providing its signature return type, and **throws** clause (if any), but does not provide an implementation. The declaration of an **abstract** method *m* must appear directly within an **abstract** class (call it *A*) unless it occurs within an enum otherwise a compile-time error results. Every subclass of *A* that is not **abstract** must provide an implementation for *m*, or a compile-time error occurs.

It is a compile-time error for a **private** method to be declared **abstract**. It would be impossible for a subclass to implement a **private abstract** method, because **private** methods are not inherited by subclasses; therefore such a method could never be used.

It is a compile-time error for a **static** method to be declared **abstract**. It is a compile-time error for a **final** method to be declared **abstract**. An **abstract** class can override an **abstract** method by providing another **abstract** method declaration.

This can provide a place to put a documentation comment, to refine the return type, or to declare that the set of checked exceptions that can be thrown by that method, when it is implemented by its subclasses, is to be more limited. For example, consider this code:

```
class BufferEmpty extends Exception {
    BufferEmpty() {super();}
    BufferEmpty(String s) {super(s);}
}
class BufferError extends Exception {
    BufferError() {super();}
    BufferError(String s) {super(s);}
}
public interface Buffer {
    char get() throws BufferEmpty, BufferError;
}
public abstract class InfiniteBuffer implements
    Buffer {
    public abstract char get() throws
    BufferError;
}
```

The overriding declaration of method **`get`** in class **`InfiniteBuffer`** states that method **`get`** in any subclass of **`InfiniteBuffer`** never throws a **`BufferEmpty`** exception, putatively because it generates the data in the buffer, and thus can never run out of data.

An instance method that is not **`abstract`** can be overridden by an **`abstract`** method. For example, we can declare an **`abstract`** class **`Point`** that requires its subclasses to implement **`toString`** if they are to be complete, instantiable classes:

```
abstract class Point {
    int x, y;
    public abstract String toString();
}
This abstract declaration of toString overrides
    the non-abstract toString method of class
    Object. (Class Object is the implicit direct
    superclass of class Point.) Adding the code:
class ColoredPoint extends Point {
    int colour;
```

```
    public String toString() {
        return super.toString() + ": colour "
    + colour;// error
    }
}
```

results in a compile-time error because the invocation `super.toString()` refers to method `toString` in class `Point`, which is `abstract` and therefore cannot be invoked. Method `toString` of class `Object` can be made available to class `ColoredPoint` only if class `Point` explicitly makes it available through some other method, as in:

```
abstract class Point {
    int x, y;
    public abstract String toString();
    protected String objString() { return
    super.toString(); }
}
class ColoredPoint extends Point {
    int color;
    public String toString() {
        return objString() + ": color " +
    color;    // correct
    }
}
```

STATIC METHODS

A method that is declared `static` is called a *class method*. A class method is always invoked without reference to a particular object. An attempt to reference the current object using the keyword `this` or the keyword `super` or to reference the type parametres of any surrounding declaration in the body of a class method results in a compile-time error.

It is a compile-time error for a `static` method to be declared `abstract`. A method that is not declared `static` is called an *instance method*, and sometimes called a non-`static` method. An instance method is always invoked with respect to an object, which becomes the current object to which the keywords `this` and `super` refer during execution of the method body.

FINAL METHODS

A method can be declared **`final`** to prevent subclasses from overriding or hiding it. It is a compile-time error to attempt to override or hide a **`final`** method. A **`private`** method and all methods declared immediately within a **`final`** class behave as if they are **`final`**, since it is impossible to override them. It is a compile-time error for a **`final`** method to be declared **`abstract`**. At run time, a machine-code generator or optimizer can "inline" the body of a **`final`** method, replacing an invocation of the method with the code in its body.

The inlining process must preserve the semantics of the method invocation. In particular, if the target of an instance method invocation is **`null`**, then a **`NullPointerException`** must be thrown even if the method is inlined. The compiler must ensure that the exception will be thrown at the correct point, so that the actual arguments to the method will be seen to have been evaluated in the correct order prior to the method invocation.

Consider the example:

```
final class Point {
    int x, y;
    void move(int dx, int dy) {x += dx; y +=
    dy;}
}
class Test {
    public static void main(String[] args) {
          Point[] p = new Point[100];
          for (int i = 0; i < p.length; i++) {
                p[i] = new Point();
                p[i].move(i, p.length-1-i);
          }
    }
}
```

Here, inlining the method move of class Point in method main would transform the for loop to

the form:

```
        for (int i = 0; i < p.length; i++) {
                p[i] = new Point();
                Point pi = p[i];
                int j = p.length-1-i;
                pi.x += i;
                pi.y += j;
        }
```

The loop might then be subject to further optimizations. Such inlining cannot be done at compile time unless it can be guaranteed that `Test` and `Point` will always be recompiled together, so that whenever `Point`-and specifically its `move` method-changes, the code for `Test.main` will also be updated.

NATIVE METHODS

A method that is `native` is implemented in platform-dependent code, typically written in another programming language such as C, C++, FORTRAN,or assembly language. The body of a `native` method is given as a semicolon only, indicating that the implementation is omitted, instead of a block.

A compile-time error occurs if a `native` method is declared `abstract`.

For example, the class `RandomAccessFile` of the package `java.io` might declare the following `native` methods:

```
package java.io;
public class RandomAccessFile
   implements DataOutput, DataInput
{  ...
   public native void open(String name, boolean
   writeable)
        throws IOException;
   public native int readBytes(byte[] b, int
   off, int len)
        throws IOException;
   public native void writeBytes(byte[] b, int
   off, int len)
        throws IOException;
```

```
    public native long getFilePointer() throws
    IOException;
    public native void seek(long pos) throws
    IOException;
    public native long length() throws
    IOException;
    public native void close() throws
    IOException;
}
```

STRICTFP METHODS

The effect of the **strictfp** modifier is to make all **float** or **double** expressions within the method body be explicitly FP-strict.

SYNCHRONIZED METHODS

A **synchronized** method acquires a monitor before it executes. For a class (**static**) method, the monitor associated with the **Class** object for the method's class is used. For an instance method, the monitor associated with **this** (the object for which the method was invoked) is used.

These are the same locks that can be used by the **synchronized** statement; thus, the code:

```
class Test {
    int count;
    synchronized void bump() { count++; }
    static int classCount;
    static synchronized void classBump() {
        classCount++;
    }
}
```

has exactly the same effect as:

```
class BumpTest {
    int count;
    void bump() {
        synchronized (this) {
            count++;
        }
```

```
    }
    static int classCount;
    static void classBump() {
        try {
        s y n c h r o n i z e d
    (Class.forName("BumpTest")) {
                classCount++;
            }
        } catch (ClassNotFoundException e) {
        ...
        }
    }
}
```

The more elaborate example:

```
public class Box {
    private Object boxContents;
    public synchronized Object get() {
        Object contents = boxContents;
        boxContents = null;
        return contents;
    }
    public synchronized boolean put(Object
    contents) {
        if (boxContents != null)
            return false;
        boxContents = contents;
        return true;
    }
}
```

defines a class which is designed for concurrent use. Each instance of the class **Box** has an instance variable **boxContents** that can hold a reference to any object. You can put an object in a **Box** by invoking **put**, which returns **false** if the box is already full. You can get something out of a **Box** by invoking **get**, which returns a null reference if the box is empty.

If **put** and **get** were not **synchronized**, and two threads were executing methods for the same instance of **Box** at the same time, then the code could misbehave. It might, for example, lose track of an object because two invocations to `put` occurred at the same time.

GENERIC METHODS

A method is *generic* if it declares one or more type variables. These type variables are known as the *formal type parametres* of the method. The form of the formal type parametre list is identical to a type parametre list of a class or interface.

The scope of a method's type parametre is the entire declaration of the method, including the type parametre section itself. Therefore, type parametres can appear as parts of their own bounds, or as bounds of other type parametres declared in the same section.

Type parametres of generic methods need not be provided explicitly when a generic method is invoked. Instead, they are almost always inferred.

METHOD RETURN TYPE

The return type of a method declares the type of value a method returns, if it returns a value, or states that the method is `void`. A method declaration d_1 with return type R_1 is return-type-substitutable for another method d_2 with return type R_2, if and only if the following conditions hold:

- If R_1 is a primitive type, then R_2 is identical to R_1.
- If R_1 is a reference type then:
  - R_1 is either a subtype of R_2 or R_1 can be converted to a subtype of R_2 by unchecked conversion or
  - $R_1 = | R_2 |$.
- If R_1 is void then R_2 is void.

Discussion: The notion of return-type substitutability summarizes the ways in which return types may vary among methods that override each other.

Note that this definition supports *covariant returns* - that is, the specialization of the return type to a subtype (but only for reference types).

Also note that unchecked conversions are allowed as well.

This is unsound, and requires an unchecked warning whenever it is used; it is a special allowance is made to allow smooth migration from non-generic to generic code.

METHOD THROWS

A *throws clause* is used to declare any checked exceptions that can result from the execution of a method or constructor:

```
Throws:
    throws ExceptionTypeList
ExceptionTypeList:
    ExceptionType
    ExceptionTypeList , ExceptionType
ExceptionType:
    ClassType
    TypeVariable
```

A compile-time error occurs if any *ExceptionType* mentioned in a **throws** clause is not a subtype of **Throwable**. It is permitted but not required to mention other (unchecked) exceptions in a **throws** clause.

For each checked exception that can result from execution of the body of a method or constructor, a compile-time error occurs unless that exception type or a supertype of that exception type is mentioned in a **throws** clause in the declaration of the method or constructor. The requirement to declare checked exceptions allows the compiler to ensure that code for handling such error conditions has been included. Methods or constructors that fail to handle exceptional conditions thrown as checked exceptions will normally result in a compile-time error because of the lack of a proper exception type in a **throws** clause.

The Java programming language thus encourages a programming style where rare and otherwise truly exceptional conditions are documented in this way. The predefined exceptions that are not checked in this way are those for which declaring every possible occurrence would be unimaginably inconvenient:

- Exceptions that are represented by the subclasses of class Error, for example OutOfMemoryError, are thrown due to a failure in or of the virtual machine. Many of these are the result of linkage failures and can occur at unpredictable points in the execution of a program. Sophisticated programs may yet wish to catch and attempt to recover from some of these conditions.

- The exceptions that are represented by the subclasses of the class RuntimeException, for example NullPointerException, result from run—time integrity checks and are thrown either directly from the program or in library routines. It is beyond the scope of the Java programming language, and perhaps beyond the state of the art, to include sufficient information in the program to reduce to a manageable number the places where these can be proven not to occur.

A method that overrides or hides another method, including methods that implement **abstract** methods defined in interfaces, may not be declared to throw more checked exceptions than the overridden or hidden method.

More precisely, suppose that *B* is a class or interface, and *A* is a superclass or superinterface of *B*, and a method declaration *n* in *B* overrides or hides a method declaration *m* in *A*. If *n* has a **throws** clause that mentions any checked exception types, then *m* must have a **throws** clause, and for every checked exception type listed in the **throws** clause of *n*, that same exception class or one of its supertypes must occur in the erasure of the **throws** clause of *m*; otherwise, a compile-time error occurs.

If the unerased **throws** clause of *m* does not contain a supertype of each exception type in the **throws** clause of *n*, an unchecked warning must be issued.

Discussion: Type variables are allowed in throws lists even though they are not allowed in catch clauses.

```
interface PrivilegedExceptionAction<E
extends Exception> {
  void run() throws E;
}
```

```
class AccessController {
  public static <E extends Exception>'
   Object do Privileged (Privileged Exception
   Action <E> action) throws E
  {... }
}
class Test {
  public static void main(String[] args) {
   try {
      AccessController.doPrivileged(
         new Privileged Exception Action<File
   Not Found Exception>() {
                public void run() throws
   FileNotFoundException
         {... delete a file...}
       });
   } catch (FileNotFoundException f) {...} //
   do something
  }
}
```

METHOD BODY

A *method body* is either a block of code that implements the method or simply a semicolon, indicating the lack of an implementation. The body of a method must be a semicolon if and only if the method is either **abstract** or **native**.

```
MethodBody:
   Block
   ;
```

A compile-time error occurs if a method declaration is either **abstract** or **native** and has a block for its body. A compile-time error occurs if a method declaration is neither **abstract** nor **native** and has a semicolon for its body.

If an implementation is to be provided for a method declared **void**, but the implementation requires no executable code, the method body should be written as a block that contains no statements: "**{ }**". If a method is declared **void**, then its body must not contain any **return** statement that has an *Expression*. If a method is declared to have a return type, then every **`return`** statement in its body must have an *Expression*. A compile-time error occurs if the body of the method can complete normally.

In other words, a method with a return type must return only by using a return statement that provides a value return; it is not allowed to "drop off the end of its body." Note that it is possible for a method to have a declared return type and yet contain no return statements. Here is one example:

```
class DizzyDean {
    int pitch() { throw new RuntimeException("90
    mph?!"); }
}
```

INHERITANCE, OVERRIDING, AND HIDING

A class *C* *inherits* from its direct superclass and direct superinterfaces all non-private methods (whether **`abstract`** or not) of the superclass and superinterfaces that are public, protected or declared with default access in the same package as *C* and are neither overridden nor hidden by a declaration in the class.

OVERRIDING (BY INSTANCE METHODS)

An instance method *m1* declared in a class *C* *overrides* another instance method, *m2*, declared in class *A* iff all of the following are true:

1. C is a subclass of *A*.
2. The signature of *m1* is a subsignature of the signature of *m2*.
3. Either
   - *m2* is public, protected or declared with default access in the same package as *C*, or
   - *m1* overrides a method *m3*, *m3* distinct from *m1*, *m3* distinct from *m2*, such that *m3* overrides *m2*.

Moreover, if *m1* is not **`abstract`**, then *m1* is said to *implement* any and all declarations of **`abstract`** methods that it overrides.

Discussion: The signature of an overriding method may

differ from the overridden one if a formal parametre in one of the methods has raw type, while the corresponding parametre in the other has a parametreized type. The rules allow the signature of the overriding method to differ from the overridden one, to accommodate migration of pre-existing code to take advantage of genericity. A compile-time error occurs if an instance method overrides a `static` method. In this respect, overriding of methods differs from hiding of fields, for it is permissible for an instance variable to hide a `static` variable.

An overridden method can be accessed by using a method invocation expression that contains the keyword `super`. Note that a qualified name or a cast to a superclass type is not effective in attempting to access an overridden method; in this respect, overriding of methods differs from hiding of fields. The presence or absence of the `strictfp` modifier has absolutely no effect on the rules for overriding methods and implementing abstract methods.

For example, it is permitted for a method that is not FP-strict to override an FP-strict method and it is permitted for an FP-strict method to override a method that is not FP-strict.

HIDING (BY CLASS METHODS)

If a class declares a `static` method *m*, then the declaration *m* is said to *hide* any method *m'*, where the signature of *m* is a subsignature of the signature of *m'*, in the superclasses and superinterfaces of the class that would otherwise be accessible to code in the class. A compile-time error occurs if a `static` method hides an instance method.

In this respect, hiding of methods differs from hiding of fields, for it is permissible for a `static` variable to hide an instance variable. Hiding is also distinct from shadowing and obscuring. A hidden method can be accessed by using a qualified name or by using a method invocation expression that contains the keyword `super` or a cast to a superclass type. In this respect, hiding of methods is similar to hiding of fields.

REQUIREMENTS IN OVERRIDING AND HIDING

If a method declaration d_1 with return type R_1 overrides or hides the declaration of another method d_2 with return type R_2, then d_1 must be return-type substitutable for d_2, or a compile-time error occurs. Furthermore, if R_1 is not a subtype of R_2, an unchecked warning must be issued. A method declaration must not have a **throws** clause that conflicts with that of any method that it overrides or hides; otherwise, a compile-time error occurs.

Discussion: The rules above allow for *covariant return types* - refining the return type of a method when overriding it. For example, the following declarations are legal although they were illegal in prior versions of the Java programming language:

```
class C implements Cloneable {
   C copy() { return (C)clone(); }
}
class D extends C implements Cloneable {
   D copy() { return (D)clone(); }
}
```

The relaxed rule for overriding also allows one to relax the conditions on abstract classes implementing interfaces.

Discussion

```
Consider
class StringSorter {
// takes a collection of strings and converts
    it to a sortedlist
    List toList(Collection c) {...}
}
and assume that someone subclasses
    StringCollector
class Overrider extends StringSorter{
    List toList(Collection c) {...}
}
Now, at some point the author of StringSorter
    decides to generify the code
class StringSorter {
// takes a collection of strings and converts
    it to a list
    List<String> toList(Collection<String> c)
```

```
    {...}
}
```

An unchecked warning would be given when compiling `Overrider` against the new definition of `StringSorter` because the return type of `Overrider.toList()` is `List`, which is not a subtype of the return type of the overridden method, `List<String>`.

In these respects, overriding of methods differs from hiding of fields, for it is permissible for a field to hide a field of another type.

It is a compile time error if a type declaration *T* has a member method m_1 and there exists a method m_2 declared in *T* or a supertype of *T* such that all of the following conditions hold:

- m_1 and m_2 have the same name.
- m_2 is accessible from *T*.
- The signature of m_1 is not a subsignature of the signature of m_2.
- m_1 or some method m_1 overrides (directly or indirectly) has the same erasure as m_2 or some method m_2 overrides (directly or indirectly).

Discussion: These restrictions are necessary because generics are implemented via erasure.

The rule above implies that methods declared in the same class with the same name must have different erasures. It also implies that a type declaration cannot implement or extend two distinct invocations of the same generic interface. Here are some further examples.

A class cannot have two member methods with the same name and type erasure.

```
class C<T> { T id (T x) {...} }
class D extends C<String> {
    Object id(Object x) {...}
}
```

This is illegal since `D.id(Object)` is a member of `D`, `C<String>.id(String)` is declared in a supertype of `D` and:

- The two methods have the same name, id
- C<String>.id(String) is accessible to D

- The signature of D.id(Object) is not a subsignature of that of C<String>.id(String)
- The two methods have the same erasure

Discussion: Two different methods of a class may not override methods with the same erasure.

```
class C<T> { T id (T x) {...} }
interface I<T> { Tid(T x); }
class D extends C<String> implements I<Integer>
   {
   String id(String x) {...}
   Integer id(Integer x) {...}
```

This is also illegal, since `D.id(String)` is a member of `D`, `D.id(Integer)` is declared in `D` and:

- The two methods have the same name, id
- The two methods have different signatures.
- D.id(Integer) is accessible to D
- D.id(String) overrides C<String>.id(String) and D.id(Integer) overrides I.id(Integer) yet the two overridden methods have the same erasure

The access modifier of an overriding or hiding method must provide at least as much access as the overridden or hidden method, or a compile-time error occurs. In more detail:

- If the overridden or hidden method is public, then the overriding or hiding method must be public; otherwise, a compile-time error occurs.
- If the overridden or hidden method is protected, then the overriding or hiding method must be protected or public; otherwise, a compile-time error occurs.
- If the overridden or hidden method has default access, then the overriding or hiding method must not be private; otherwise, a compile-time error occurs.

Note that a `private` method cannot be hidden or overridden in the technical sense of those terms. This means that a subclass can declare a method with the same signature as a `private` method in one of its superclasses, and there is no requirement that the return type or `throws` clause of such a method bear any relationship to those of the `private` method in the superclass.

INHERITING METHODS WITH OVERRIDE-EQUIVALENT SIGNATURES

It is possible for a class to inherit multiple methods with override-equivalent signatures. It is a compile time error if a class C inherits a concrete method whose signatures is a subsignature of another concrete method inherited by C.

Discussion: This can happen, if a superclass is parametric, and it has two methods that were distinct in the generic declaration, but have the same signature in the particular invocation used.

Otherwise, there are two possible cases:

- If one of the inherited methods is not abstract, then there are two subcases:
  - If the method that is not abstract is static, a compile-time error occurs.
  - Otherwise, the method that is not abstract is considered to override, and therefore to implement, all the other methods on behalf of the class that inherits it. If the signature of the non-abstract method is not a subsignature of each of the other inherited methods an unchecked warning must be issued. A compile-time error also occurs if the return type of the non-abstract method is not return type substitutable for each of the other inherited methods. If the return type of the non-abstract method is not a subtype of the return type of any of the other inherited methods, an unchecked warning must be issued. Moreover, a compile-time error occurs if the inherited method that is not abstract has a throws clause that conflicts with that of any other of the inherited methods.
- If all the inherited methods are abstract, then the class is necessarily an abstract class and is considered to inherit all the abstract methods. A compile-time error occurs if, for any two such inherited methods, one of the methods is not return type substitutable for

the other (The throws clauses do not cause errors in this case.)

There might be several paths by which the same method declaration might be inherited from an interface. This fact causes no difficulty and never, of itself, results in a compile-time error.

OVERLOADING

If two methods of a class (whether both declared in the same class, or both inherited by a class, or one declared and one inherited) have the same name but signatures that are not override-equivalent, then the method name is said to be *overloaded*. This fact causes no difficulty and never of itself results in a compile-time error. There is no required relationship between the return types or between the `throws` clauses of two methods with the same name, unless their signatures are override-equivalent. Methods are overridden on a signature-by-signature basis. If, for example, a class declares two `public` methods with the same name, and a subclass overrides one of them, the subclass still inherits the other method.

When a method is invoked, the number of actual arguments (and any explicit type arguments) and the compile-time types of the arguments are used, at compile time, to determine the signature of the method that will be invoked. If the method that is to be invoked is an instance method, the actual method to be invoked will be determined at run time, using dynamic method lookup.

METHOD DECLARATIONS

The following examples illustrate some (possibly subtle) points about method declarations.

Overriding

In the example:

```
class Point {
   int x = 0, y = 0;
   void move(int dx, int dy) { x += dx; y +=
   dy; }
```

```
}
class SlowPoint extends Point {
    int xLimit, yLimit;
    void move(int dx, int dy) {
    super.move(limit(dx, xLimit), limit(dy,
    yLimit));
    }
    static int limit(int d, int limit) {
    return d > limit ? limit : d < -limit ? -
    limit : d;
    }
}
```

the class `SlowPoint` overrides the declarations of method `move` of class `Point` with its own `move` method, which limits the distance that the point can move on each invocation of the method. When the `move` method is invoked for an instance of class `SlowPoint`, the overriding definition in class `SlowPoint` will always be called, even if the reference to the `SlowPoint` object is taken from a variable whose type is `Point`.

Overloading, Overriding, and Hiding

In the example:

```
class Point {
    int x = 0, y = 0;
    void move(int dx, int dy) { x += dx; y +=
    dy; }
    int color;
}
class RealPoint extends Point {
    float x = 0.0f, y = 0.0f;
    void move(int dx, int dy) { move((float)dx,
    (float)dy); }
    void move(float dx, float dy) { x += dx; y
    += dy; }
}
```

the class `RealPoint` hides the declarations of the `int` instance variables `x` and `y` of class `Point` with its own `float` instance variables `x` and `y`, and overrides the method `move` of class

Point with its own **move** method. It also overloads the name **move** with another method with a different signature.

In this example, the members of the class **RealPoint** include the instance variable **color** inherited from the class **Point**, the **float** instance variables **x** and **y** declared in **RealPoint**, and the two **move** methods declared in **RealPoint**. Which of these overloaded **move** methods of class **RealPoint** will be chosen for any particular method invocation will be determined at compile time by the overloading resolution procedure described later.

INCORRECT OVERRIDING

This example is an extended variation of that in the preceding section:

```
class Point {
    int x = 0, y = 0, color;
    void move(int dx, int dy) { x += dx; y +=
    dy; }
    int getX() { return x; }
    int getY() { return y; }
}
class RealPoint extends Point {
    float x = 0.0f, y = 0.0f;
    void move(int dx, int dy) { move((float)dx,
    (float)dy); }
    void move(float dx, float dy) { x += dx; y
    += dy; }
    float getX() { return x; }
    float getY() { return y; }
}
```

Here the class **Point** provides methods **getX** and **getY** that return the values of its fields **x** and **y**; the class **RealPoint** then overrides these methods by declaring methods with the same signature. The result is two errors at compile time, one for each method, because the return types do not match; the methods in class **Point** return values of type **int**, but the wanna-be overriding methods in class **RealPoint** return values of type **float**.

OVERRIDING VERSUS HIDING

This example corrects the errors of the example in the preceding section:

```
class Point {
    int x = 0, y = 0;
    void move(int dx, int dy) { x += dx; y +=
    dy; }
    int getX() { return x; }
    int getY() { return y; }
    int color;
}
class RealPoint extends Point {
    float x = 0.0f, y = 0.0f;
    void move(int dx, int dy) { move((float)dx,
    (float)dy); }
    void move(float dx, float dy) { x += dx; y
    += dy; }
    int getX() { return (int)Math.floor(x); }
    int getY() { return (int)Math.floor(y); }
}
```

Here the overriding methods `getX` and `getY` in class `RealPoint` have the same return types as the methods of class `Point` that they override, so this code can be successfully compiled.

Consider, then, this test program:

```
class Test {
    public static void main(String[] args) {
        RealPoint rp = new RealPoint();
        Point p = rp;
        rp.move(1.71828f, 4.14159f);
        p.move(1, -1);
        show(p.x, p.y);
        show(rp.x, rp.y);
        show(p.getX(), p.getY());
        show(rp.getX(), rp.getY());
    }
    static void show(int x, int y) {
```

```
        System.out.println("(" + x + ", " + y
    + ")");
    }
    static void show(float x, float y) {
        System.out.println("(" + x + ", " + y
    + ")");
    }
}
```

The output from this program is:

```
(0, 0)
(2.7182798, 3.14159)
(2, 3)
(2, 3)
```

The first line of output illustrates the fact that an instance of **RealPoint** actually contains the two integer fields declared in class **Point**; it is just that their names are hidden from code that occurs within the declaration of class **RealPoint** (and those of any subclasses it might have). When a reference to an instance of class **RealPoint** in a variable of type **Point** is used to access the field **x**, the integer field **x** declared in class **Point** is accessed.

The fact that its value is zero indicates that the method invocation **p.move(1, -1)** did not invoke the method **move** of class **Point**; instead, it invoked the overriding method **move** of class **RealPoint**. The second line of output shows that the field access **rp.x** refers to the field **x** declared in class **RealPoint**.

This field is of type **float**, and this second line of output accordingly displays floating-point values. Incidentally, this also illustrates the fact that the method name **show** is overloaded; the types of the arguments in the method invocation dictate which of the two definitions will be invoked.

The last two lines of output show that the method invocations **p.getX()** and **rp.getX()** each invoke the **getX** method declared in class **RealPoint**.

Indeed, there is no way to invoke the **getX** method of class **Point** for an instance of class **RealPoint** from outside the body of **RealPoint**, no matter what the type of the variable we may use to hold the reference to the object. Thus, we see that fields and methods behave differently: hiding is different from overriding.

INVOCATION OF HIDDEN CLASS METHODS

A hidden class (**static**) method can be invoked by using a reference whose type is the class that actually contains the declaration of the method. In this respect, hiding of static methods is different from overriding of instance methods. The example:

```
class Super {
    static String greeting() { return
    "Goodnight"; }
    String name() { return "Richard"; }
}
class Sub extends Super {
    static String greeting() { return "Hello";
    }
    String name() { return "Dick"; }
}
class Test {
    public static void main(String[] args) {
         Super s = new Sub();
         System.out.println(s.greeting() + ",
    " + s.name());
    }
}
```

produces the output:

```
Goodnight, Dick
```

because the invocation of **greeting** uses the type of **s**, namely **Super**, to figure out, at compile time, which class method to invoke, whereas the invocation of **name** uses the class of **s**, namely **Sub**, to figure out, at run time, which instance method to invoke.

LARGE EXAMPLE OF OVERRIDING

Overriding makes it easy for subclasses to extend the behaviour of an existing class, as shown in this example:

```
import java.io.OutputStream;
import java.io.IOException;
class BufferOutput {
    private OutputStream o;
    BufferOutput(OutputStream o) { this.o = o;
    }
    protected byte[] buf = new byte[512];
    protected int pos = 0;
    public void putchar(char c) throws
    IOException {
        if (pos == buf.length)
            flush();
        buf[pos++] = (byte)c;
    }
    public void putstr(String s) throws
    IOException {
        for (int i = 0; i < s.length(); i++)
            putchar(s.charAt(i));
    }
    public void flush() throws IOException {
        o.write(buf, 0, pos);
        pos = 0;
    }
}
class LineBufferOutput extends BufferOutput {
    LineBufferOutput(OutputStream o) { super(o);
    }
    public void putchar(char c) throws
    IOException {
        super.putchar(c);
        if (c == '\n')
            flush();
    }
}
class Test {
    public static void main(String[] args)
        throws IOException
    {
```

```
            LineBufferOutput lbo =
                    n         e
        LineBufferOutput(System.out);
            lbo.putstr("lbo\nlbo");
            System.out.print("print\n");
            lbo.putstr("\n");
        }
}
```

This example produces the output:

```
lbo
print
lbo
```

The class `BufferOutput` implements a very simple buffered version of an `OutputStream`, flushing the output when the buffer is full or `flush` is invoked. The subclass `LineBufferOutput` declares only a constructor and a single method `putchar`, which overrides the method `putchar` of `BufferOutput`. It inherits the methods `putstr` and `flush` from class `BufferOutput`.

In the `putchar` method of a `LineBufferOutput` object, if the character argument is a newline, then it invokes the `flush` method. The critical point about overriding in this example is that the method `putstr`, which is declared in class `BufferOutput`, invokes the `putchar` method defined by the current object `this`, which is not necessarily the `putchar` method declared in class `BufferOutput`.

Thus, when `putstr` is invoked in `main` using the `LineBufferOutput` object `lbo`, the invocation of `putchar` in the body of the `putstr` method is an invocation of the `putchar` of the object `lbo`, the overriding declaration of `putchar` that checks for a newline. This allows a subclass of `BufferOutput` to change the behaviour of the `putstr` method without redefining it.

Documentation for a class such as `BufferOutput`, which is designed to be extended, should clearly indicate what is the contract between the class and its subclasses, and should clearly indicate that subclasses may override the `putchar` method in this way. The implementor of the `BufferOutput` class would not, therefore, want to change the implementation of `putstr` in a future implementation of `BufferOutput` not to use the method `putchar`, because this would break the preexisting contract with subclasses.

INCORRECT OVERRIDING BECAUSE OF THROWS

This example uses the usual and conventional form for declaring a new exception type, in its declaration of the class `BadPointException`:

```
class BadPointException extends Exception {
    BadPointException() { super(); }
    BadPointException(String s) { super(s); }
}
class Point {
    int x, y;
    void move(int dx, int dy) { x += dx; y +=
    dy; }
}
class CheckedPoint extends Point {
    void move(int dx, int dy) throws
    BadPointException {
        if ((x + dx) < 0 || (y + dy) < 0)
            throw new BadPointException();
        x += dx; y += dy;
    }
}
```

This example results in a compile-time error, because the override of method `move` in class `CheckedPoint` declares that it will throw a checked exception that the `move` in class `Point` has not declared. If this were not considered an error, an invoker of the method `move` on a reference of type `Point` could find the contract between it and `Point` broken if this exception were thrown.

Removing the `throws` clause does not help:

```
class CheckedPoint extends Point {
    void move(int dx, int dy) {
        if ((x + dx) < 0 || (y + dy) < 0)
```

```
                throw new BadPointException();
            x += dx; y += dy;
        }
}
```

A different compile-time error now occurs, because the body of the method **move** cannot throw a checked exception, namely **BadPointException**, that does not appear in the **throws** clause for **move**.

MEMBER TYPE DECLARATIONS

A *member class* is a class whose declaration is directly enclosed in another class or interface declaration. Similarly, a *member interface* is an interface whose declaration is directly enclosed in another class or interface declaration. If the class declares a member type with a certain name, then the declaration of that type is said to *hide* any and all accessible declarations of member types with the same name in superclasses and superinterfaces of the class. Within a class *C*, a declaration *d* of a member type named *n* shadows the declarations of any other types named *n* that are in scope at the point where *d* occurs.

If a member class or interface declared with simple name C is directly enclosed within the declaration of a class with fully qualified name *N*, then the member class or interface has the fully qualified name *N.C*. A class inherits from its direct superclass and direct superinterfaces all the non-private member types of the superclass and superinterfaces that are both accessible to code in the class and not hidden by a declaration in the class.

A class may inherit two or more type declarations with the same name, either from two interfaces or from its superclass and an interface. A compile-time error occurs on any attempt to refer to any ambiguously inherited class or interface by its simple name

If the same type declaration is inherited from an interface by multiple paths, the class or interface is considered to be inherited only once. It may be referred to by its simple name without ambiguity.

MODIFIERS

A compile-time error occurs if a member type declaration has more than one of the access modifiers **`public`**, **`protected`**, and **`private`**. Member type declarations may have annotation modifers just like any type or member declaration.

STATIC MEMBER TYPE DECLARATIONS

The **`static`** keyword may modify the declaration of a member type *C* within the body of a non-inner class *T*. Its effect is to declare that *C* is not an inner class.

Just as a static method of *T* has no current instance of *T* in its body, *C* also has no current instance of *T*, nor does it have any lexically enclosing instances. It is a compile-time error if a **`static`** class contains a usage of a non-**`static`** member of an enclosing class. Member interfaces are always implicitly **`static`**. It is permitted but not required for the declaration of a member interface to explicitly list the **`static`** modifier.

INSTANCE INITIALIZERS

An *instance initializer* declared in a class is executed when an instance of the class is created,

```
InstanceInitializer:
    Block
```

It is compile-time error if an instance initializer of a named class can throw a checked exception unless that exception or one of its supertypes is explicitly declared in the **`throws`** clause of each constructor of its class and the class has at least one explicitly declared constructor. An instance initializer in an anonymous class can throw any exceptions.

The rules above distinguish between instance initializers in named and anonymous classes. This distinction is deliberate. A given anonymous class is only instantiated at a single point in a program. It is therefore possible to directly propagate information about what exceptions might be raised by an anonymous class' instance initializer to the surrounding expression. Named classes, on the other hand, can be instantiated in many places.

Therefore the only way to propagate information about what exceptions might be raised by an instance initializer of a named class is through the throws clauses of its constructors. It follows that a more liberal rule can be used in the case of anonymous classes. Similar comments apply to instance variable initializers. It is a compile-time error if an instance initializer cannot complete normally. If a return statement appears anywhere within an instance initializer, then a compile-time error occurs.

Use of instance variables whose declarations appear textually after the use is sometimes restricted, even though these instance variables are in scope. Instance initializers are permitted to refer to the current object this, to any type variables in scope and to use the keyword `super`

STATIC INITIALIZERS

Any *static initializers* declared in a class are executed when the class is initialized and, together with any field initializers for class variables, may be used to initialize the class variables of the class.

```
StaticInitializer:
    static Block
```

It is a compile-time error for a static initializer to be able to complete abruptly with a checked exception. It is a compile-time error if a static initializer cannot complete normally. The static initializers and class variable initializers are executed in textual order. Use of class variables whose declarations appear textually after the use is sometimes restricted, even though these class variables are in scope. If a `return` statement appears anywhere within a static initializer, then a compile-time error occurs. If the keyword `this` or any type variable defined outside the initializer or the keyword `super` appears anywhere within a static initializer, then a compile-time error occurs.

Constructor Declarations

A *constructor* is used in the creation of an object that is an instance of a class:

```
ConstructorDeclaration:
    ConstructorModifiersopt
```

```
    ConstructorDeclarator
        Throwsopt ConstructorBody
ConstructorDeclarator:
    TypeParametresopt SimpleTypeName (
    FormalParametreListopt )
```

The *SimpleTypeName* in the *ConstructorDeclarator* must be the simple name of the class that contains the constructor declaration; otherwise a compile-time error occurs. In all other respects, the constructor declaration looks just like a method declaration that has no result type.

Here is a simple example:

```
class Point {
int x, y;
Point(int x, int y) { this.x = x; this.y = y;
}
}
```

Constructors are invoked by class instance creation expressions, by the conversions and concatenations caused by the string concatenation operator + and by explicit constructor invocations from other constructors.Constructors are never invoked by method invocation expressions. Access to constructors is governed by access modifiers. This is useful, for example, in preventing instantiation by declaring an inaccessible constructor. Constructor declarations are not members. They are never inherited and therefore are not subject to hiding or overriding.

FORMAL PARAMETRES AND FORMAL TYPE PARAMETRE

The formal parametres and formal type parametres of a constructor are identical in structure and behaviour to the formal parametres of a method.

Constructor Signature

It is a compile-time error to declare two constructors with override-equivalent *signatures* in a class. It is a compile-time error to declare two constructors whose signature has the same erasure in a class.

CONSTRUCTOR MODIFIERS

```
ConstructorModifiers:
    ConstructorModifier
    ConstructorModifiers ConstructorModifier
ConstructorModifier: one of
     Annotation public protected private
```

A compile-time error occurs if the same modifier appears more than once in a constructor declaration, or if a constructor declaration has more than one of the access modifiers `public`, `protected`, and `private`. If no access modifier is specified for the constructor of a normal class, the constructor has default access. If no access modifier is specified for the constructor of an enum type, the constructor is `private`. It is a compile-time error if the constructor of an enum type is declared `public` or `protected`. If an annotation *a* on a constructor corresponds to an annotation type *T*, and *T* has a (meta-)annotation *m* that corresponds to `annotation.Target`, then *m* must have an element whose value is `annotation.ElementType.CONSTRUCTOR`, or a compile-time error occurs. Unlike methods, a constructor cannot be `abstract`, `static`, `final`, `native`, `strictfp`, or `synchronized`. A constructor is not inherited, so there is no need to declare it `final` and an `abstract` constructor could never be implemented.

A constructor is always invoked with respect to an object, so it makes no sense for a constructor to be `static`. There is no practical need for a constructor to be `synchronized`, because it would lock the object under construction, which is normally not made available to other threads until all constructors for the object have completed their work. The lack of `native` constructors is an arbitrary language design choice that makes it easy for an implementation of the Java virtual machine to verify that superclass constructors are always properly invoked during object creation.

GENERIC CONSTRUCTORS

It is possible for a constructor to be declared generic, independently of whether the class the constructor is declared in is itself generic. A constructor is *generic* if it declares one or more type variables These type variables are known as the *formal type parametres* of the constructor. The form of the formal type parametre list is identical to a type parametre list of a generic class or interface. The scope of a constructor's type parametre is the entire declaration of the constructor, including the type parametre section itself. Therefore, type parametres can appear as parts of their own bounds, or as bounds of other type parametres declared in the same section. Type parametres of generic constructor need not be provided explicitly when a generic constructor is invoked. When they are not provided.

CONSTRUCTOR THROWS

The **throws** clause for a constructor is identical in structure and behaviour to the **throws** clause for a method

The Type of a Constructor

The type of a constructor consists of its signature and the exception types given its throws clause.

CONSTRUCTOR BODY

The first statement of a constructor body may be an explicit invocation of another constructor of the same class or of the direct superclass.

```
ConstructorBody:
    { ExplicitConstructorInvocationopt
    BlockStatementsopt }
```

It is a compile-time error for a constructor to directly or indirectly invoke itself through a series of one or more explicit constructor invocations involving **this**. If the constructor is a constructor for an enum type, it is a compile-time error for it to invoke the superclass constructor explicitly.

If a constructor body does not begin with an explicit constructor invocation and the constructor being declared is not part of the primordial class **Object**, then the constructor body is implicitly assumed by the compiler to begin with a superclass constructor invocation "**super();**", an invocation of the constructor of its direct superclass that takes no arguments.

Except for the possibility of explicit constructor invocations, the body of a constructor is like the body of a method. A `return` statement may be used in the body of a constructor if it does not include an expression.

In the example:

```
class Point {
    int x, y;
    Point(int x, int y) { this.x = x; this.y =
    y; }
}
class ColoredPoint extends Point {
    static final int WHITE = 0, BLACK = 1;
    int color;
    ColoredPoint(int x, int y) {
        this(x, y, WHITE);
    }
    ColoredPoint(int x, int y, int color) {
        super(x, y);
        this.color = color;
    }
}
```

the first constructor of `ColoredPoint` invokes the second, providing an additional argument; the second constructor of `ColoredPoint` invokes the constructor of its superclass `Point`, passing along the coordinates.

EXPLICIT CONSTRUCTOR INVOCATIONS

```
ExplicitConstructorInvocation:
    NonWildTypeArgumentsopt this (
    ArgumentListopt ) ;
    NonWildTypeArgumentsopt super (
    ArgumentListopt ) ;
    Primary. NonWildTypeArgumentsopt super (
    ArgumentListopt ) ;

NonWildTypeArguments:
    < ReferenceTypeList >
ReferenceTypeList:
```

ReferenceType
ReferenceTypeList , ReferenceType

Explicit constructor invocation statements can be divided into two kinds:

- *Alternate constructor invocations* begin with the keyword this (possibly prefaced with explicit type arguments). They are used to invoke an alternate constructor of the same class.
- *Superclass constructor invocations* begin with either the keyword super (possibly prefaced with explicit type arguments) or a *Primary* expression. They are used to invoke a constructor of the direct superclass. Superclass constructor invocations may be further subdivided:
  - *Unqualified superclass constructor invocations* begin with the keyword super (possibly prefaced with explicit type arguments).
  - *Qualified superclass constructor invocations* begin with a *Primary* expression. They allow a subclass constructor to explicitly specify the newly created object's immediately enclosing instance with respect to the direct superclass.This may be necessary when the superclass is an inner class.

Here is an example of a qualified superclass constructor invocation:

```
class Outer {
    class Inner{}
}
class ChildOfInner extends Outer.Inner {
    ChildOfInner(){(new Outer()).super();}
}
```

An explicit constructor invocation statement in a constructor body may not refer to any instance variables or instance methods declared in this class or any superclass, or use **this** or **super** in any expression; otherwise, a compile-time error occurs. For example, if the first constructor of **ColoredPoint** in the example above were changed to:

```
ColoredPoint(int x, int y) {
```

```
    this(x, y, color);
}
```

then a compile-time error would occur, because an instance variable cannot be used within a superclass constructor invocation. An explicit constructor invocation statement can throw an exception type *E* iff either.

- Some subexpression of the constructor invocation's parametre list can throw *E*; or
- *E* is declared in the throws clause of the constructor that is invoked.

If an anonymous class instance creation expression appears within an explicit constructor invocation statement, then the anonymous class may not refer to any of the enclosing instances of the class whose constructor is being invoked.

Example:

```
class Top {
    int x;
    class Dummy {
        Dummy(Object o) {}
    }
    class Inside extends Dummy {
        Inside() {
            super(new Object() { int r = x;
    }); // error
        }
        Inside(final int y) {
            super(new Object() { int r = y;
    }); // correct
        }
    }
}
```

Let *C* be the class being instantiated, let *S* be the direct superclass of *C*, and let *i* be the instance being created. The evaluation of an explicit constructor invocation proceeds as follows:

- First, if the constructor invocation statement is a superclass constructor invocation, then the immediately enclosing instance of *i* with respect to *S* (if any) must be determined. Whether or not *i* has an immediately enclosing instance with respect to *S* is determined by the superclass constructor invocation as follows:

- If *S* is not an inner class, or if the declaration of *S* occurs in a static context, no immediately enclosing instance of *i* with respect to *S* exists. A compile-time error occurs if the superclass constructor invocation is a qualified superclass constructor invocation.
- Otherwise:

- If the superclass constructor invocation is qualified, then the *Primary* expression *p* immediately preceding ".super" is evaluated. If the primary expression evaluates to null, a NullPointerException is raised, and the superclass constructor invocation completes abruptly. Otherwise, the result of this evaluation is the immediately enclosing instance of *i* with respect to *S*. Let *O* be the immediately lexically enclosing class of *S*; it is a compile-time error if the type of *p* is not *O* or a subclass of *O*.
- Otherwise:
- If *S* is a local class, then let *O* be the innermost lexically enclosing class of *S*. Let *n* be an integer such that *O* is the *n*th lexically enclosing class of *C*. The immediately enclosing instance of *i* with respect to *S* is the *n*th lexically enclosing instance of this.
- Otherwise, *S* is an inner member class. It is a compile-time error if *S* is not a member of a lexically enclosing class, or of a superclass or superinterface thereof. Let *O* be the innermost lexically enclosing class of which *S* is a member, and let *n* be an integer such that *O* is the *n*th lexically enclosing class of *C*. The immediately enclosing instance of *i* with respect to *S* is the *n*th lexically enclosing instance of this.
- Second, the arguments to the constructor are evaluated, left-to-right, as in an ordinary method invocation.
- Next, the constructor is invoked.

- Finally, if the constructor invocation statement is a superclass constructor invocation and the constructor invocation statement completes normally, then all instance variable initializers of *C* and all instance initializers of *C* are executed. If an instance initializer or instance variable initializer *I* textually precedes another instance initializer or instance variable initializer *J*, then *I* is executed before *J*. This action is performed regardless of whether the superclass constructor invocation actually appears as an explicit constructor invocation statement or is provided automatically. An alternate constructor invocation does not perform this additional implicit action.

CONSTRUCTOR OVERLOADING

Overloading of constructors is identical in behaviour to overloading of methods. The overloading is resolved at compile time by each class instance creation expression.

DEFAULT CONSTRUCTOR

If a class contains no constructor declarations, then a *default constructor* that takes no parametres is automatically provided:

- If the class being declared is the primordial class Object, then the default constructor has an empty body.
- Otherwise, the default constructor takes no parametres and simply invokes the superclass constructor with no arguments.

A compile-time error occurs if a default constructor is provided by the compiler but the superclass does not have an accessible constructor that takes no arguments. A default constructor has no `throws` clause. It follows that if the nullary constructor of the superclass has a `throws` clause, then a compile-time error will occur.

In an enum type, the default constructor is implicitly `private`. Otherwise, if the class is declared `public`, then the default constructor is implicitly given the access modifier `public`; if the class is declared `protected`, then the default constructor is implicitly given the access modifier **protected**; if the class is declared **private**, then the default constructor is implicitly given the access modifier **private**; otherwise, the default constructor has the default access implied by no access modifier.

Thus, the example:

```
public class Point {
    int x, y;
}
is equivalent to the declaration:
public class Point {
    int x, y;
    public Point() { super(); }
}
```

where the default constructor is **public** because the class **Point** is **public**. The rule that the default constructor of a class has the same access modifier as the class itself is simple and intuitive. Note, however, that this does not imply that the constructor is accessible whenever the class is accessible.

```
package p1;
public class Outer {
    protected class Inner{}
}
package p2;
class SonOfOuter extends p1.Outer {
    void foo() {
        new Inner(); // compile-time access
    error
    }
}
```

The constructor for **Inner** is protected. However, the constructor is protected relative to **Inner**, while **Inner** is protected relative to **Outer**.

So, **Inner** is accessible in **SonOfOuter**, since it is a subclass of **Outer**. **Inner**'s constructor is not accessible in **SonOfOuter**, because the class **SonOfOuter** is not a subclass of **Inner**! Hence, even though **Inner** is accessible, its default constructor is not.

PREVENTING INSTANTIATION OF A CLASS

A class can be designed to prevent code outside the class declaration from creating instances of the class by declaring at least one constructor, to prevent the creation of an implicit constructor, and declaring all constructors to be **`private`**. A **`public`** class can likewise prevent the creation of instances outside its package by declaring at least one constructor, to prevent creation of a default constructor with **`public`** access, and declaring no constructor that is **`public`**.

Thus, in the example:

```
class ClassOnly {
    private ClassOnly() { }
    static String just = "only the lonely";
}
```

the class ClassOnly cannot be instantiated, while in the example:

```
package just;
public class PackageOnly {
    PackageOnly() { }
    String[] justDesserts = { "cheesecake", "ice
    cream" };
}
```

the class **`PackageOnly`** can be instantiated only within the package **`just`**, in which it is declared.

ENUMS

An enum declaration has the form:

```
EnumDeclaration:
    ClassModifiersopt enum Identifier
    Interfacesopt EnumBody

EnumBody:
    {         EnumConstantsopt        ,opt
    EnumBodyDeclarationsopt }
```

The body of an enum type may contain *enum constants*. An enum constant defines an instance of the enum type. An enum type has no instances other than those defined by its enum constants.

Discussion: It is a compile-time error to attempt to explicitly instantiate an enum type.The final clone method in Enum ensures that enum constants can never be cloned, and the special treatment by the serialization mechanism ensures that duplicate instances are never created as a result of deserialization. Reflective instantiation of enum types is prohibited.

Together, these four things ensure that no instances of an enum type exist beyond those defined by the enum constants. Because there is only one instance of each enum constant, it is permissible to use the == operator in place of the `equals` method when comparing two object references if it is known that at least one of them refers to an enum constant. (The `equals` method in `Enum` is a final method that merely invokes `super.equals` on its argument and returns the result, thus performing an identity comparison.)

```
EnumConstants:
    EnumConstant
    EnumConstants , EnumConstant
EnumConstant:
    Annotations Identifier Argumentsopt
    ClassBodyopt
Arguments:
    ( ArgumentListopt )
EnumBodyDeclarations:
    ; ClassBodyDeclarationsopt
```

An enum constant may be preceded by annotation modifiers. If an annotation *a* on an enum constant corresponds to an annotation type *T*, and *T* has a (meta-)annotation *m* that corresponds to `annotation.Target`, then *m* must have an element whose value is `annotation.ElementType.FIELD`, or a compile-time error occurs.

An enum constant may be followed by arguments, which are passed to the constructor of the enum type when the constant is created during class initialization as described later in this section.

The constructor to be invoked is chosen using the normal overloading rules.If the arguments are omitted, an empty argument list is assumed. If the enum type has no constructor declarations, a parametreless default constructor is provided (which matches the implicit empty argument list). This default constructor is **`private`**. The optional class body of an enum constant implicitly defines an anonymous class declaration that extends the immediately enclosing enum type. The class body is governed by the usual rules of anonymous classes; in particular it cannot contain any constructors.

Discussion : Instance methods declared in these class bodies are may be invoked outside the enclosing enum type only if they override accessible methods in the enclosing enum type. Enum types must not be declared abstract; doing so will result in a compile-time error. It is a compile-time error for an enum type *E* to have an abstract method *m* as a member unless *E* has one or more enum constants, and all of *E*'s enum constants have class bodies that provide concrete implementations of *m*. It is a compile-time error for the class body of an enum constant to declare an abstract method.

An enum type is implicitly **`final`** unless it contains at least one enum constant that has a class body. In any case, it is a compile-time error to explicitly declare an enum type to be `final`. Nested enum types are implicitly **`static`**. It is permissable to explicitly declare a nested enum type to be **`static`**.

Discussion: This implies that it is impossible to define a local enum, or to define an enum in an inner class. Any constructor or member declarations within an enum declaration apply to the enum type exactly as if they had been present in the class body of a normal class declaration unless explicitly stated otherwise.

The direct superclass of an enum type named *E* is **`Enum<E>`**. In addition to the members it inherits from **`Enum<E>`**, for each declared enum constant with the name *n* the enum type has an implicitly declared public **`static final`** field named *n* of type *E*. These fields are considered to be declared in the same order as the corresponding enum constants, before any static fields explicitly declared in the enum type.

Each such field is initialized to the enum constant that

corresponds to it. Each such field is also considered to be annotated by the same annotations as the corresponding enum constant. The enum constant is said to be created when the corresponding field is initialized. It is a compile-time error for an enum to declare a finalizer. An instance of an enum may never be finalized. In addition, if *E* is the name of an enum type, then that type has the following implicitly declared static methods:

```
/**
*   Returns an array containing the constants
    of this enum
*   type, in the order they're declared.  This
    method may be
*   used to iterate over the constants as
    follows:
*
*   for(E c : E.values())
*   System.out.println(c);
*
*   @return an array containing the constants
    of this enum
*   type, in the order they're declared
*/
    public static E[] values();
/**
*   Returns the enum constant of this type with
    the specified
*   name.
*   The string must match exactly an identifier
    used to declare
*   an enum constant in this type.  (Extraneous
    whitespace
*   characters are not permitted.)
*
*   @return the enum constant with the specified
    name
*   @throws IllegalArgumentException if this
```

```
    enum type has no
*   constant with the specified name
*/
public static E valueOf(String name);
```

Discussion: It follows that enum type declarations cannot contain fields that conflict with the enum constants, and cannot contain methods that conflict with the automatically generated methods (`values()` and `valueOf(String)`) or methods that override the final methods in `Enum`: (`equals(Object)`, `hashCode()`, `clone()`, `compareTo(Object)`, `name()`, `ordinal()`, and `getDeclaringClass()`).

It is a compile-time error to reference a static field of an enum type that is not a compile-time constant from constructors, instance initializer blocks, or instance variable initializer expressions of that type. It is a compile-time error for the constructors, instance initializer blocks, or instance variable initializer expressions of an enum constant *e* to refer to itself or to an enum constant of the same type that is declared to the right of *e*. Discussion : Without this rule, apparently reasonable code would fail at run time due to the initialization circularity inherent in enum types. (A circularity exists in any class with a "self-typed" static field.) Here is an example of the sort of code that would fail:

```
enum Color {
        RED, GREEN, BLUE;
       static final Map<String,Color> colorMap
   =
         new HashMap<String,Color>();
        Color() {
             colorMap.put(toString(), this);
        }
   }
```

Static initialization of this enum type would throw a NullPointerException because the static variable colorMap is uninitialized when the constructors for the enum constants run. The restriction above ensures that such code won't compile.

Note that the example can easily be refactored to work properly:

```
enum Color {
```

```
        RED, GREEN, BLUE;
      static final Map<String,Color> colorMap
  =
        new HashMap<String,Color>();
      static {
          for (Color c : Color.values())
             colorMap.put(c.toString(), c);
      }
  }
```

The refactored version is clearly correct, as static initialization occurs top to bottom.

Discussion: Here is program with a nested enum declaration that uses an enhanced for loop to iterate over the constants in the enum:

```
public class Example1 {
   public enum Season { WINTER, SPRING, SUMMER,
    FALL }
    public static void main(String[] args) {
        for (Season s : Season.values())
            System.out.println(s);
    }
}
```

Running this program produces the following output:

```
WINTER
SPRING
SUMMER
FALL
```

Here is a program illustrating the use of `EnumSet` to work with subranges:

```
import java.util.*;
public class Example2 {
      enum Day { MONDAY, TUESDAY, WEDNESDAY,
    THURSDAY, FRIDAY, SATURDAY, SUNDAY
}

    public static void main(String[] args) {
        System.out.print("Weekdays: ");
```

```
        for (Day d : EnumSet.range(Day.MONDAY,
    Day.FRIDAY))
            System.out.print(d + " ");
        System.out.println();
    }
}
```

Running this program produces the following output:

Weekdays: MONDAY TUESDAY WEDNESDAY THURSDAY FRIDAY

EnumSet contains a rich family of static factories, so this technique can be generalized to work non-contiguous subsets as well as subranges. At first glance, it might appear wasteful to generate an **EnumSet** for a single iteration, but they are so cheap that this is the recommended idiom for iteration over a subrange. Internally, an **EnumSet** is represented with a single long assuming the enum type has 64 or fewer elements.

Here is a slightly more complex enum declaration for an enum type with an explicit instance field and an accessor for this field. Each member has a different value in the field, and the values are passed in via a constructor. In this example, the field represents the value, in cents, of an American coin. Note, however, that their are no restrictions on the type or number of parametres that may be passed to an enum constructor.

```
public enum Coin {
    PENNY(1), NICKEL(5), DIME(10), QUARTER(25);
     Coin(int value) { this.value = value; }
     private final int value;
     public int value() { return value; }
}
```

Switch statements are useful for simulating the addition of a method to an enum type from outside the type. This example "adds" a color method to the **Coin** type, and prints a table of coins, their values, and their colors.

```
public class CoinTest {
    public static void main(String[] args) {
        for (Coin c : Coin.values())
            System.out.println(c + ":       "+
    c.value() +"¢    " + color(c));
```

```
    }
    private enum CoinColor { COPPER, NICKEL,
    SILVER }
    private static CoinColor color(Coin c) {
        switch(c) {
          case PENNY:
            return CoinColor.COPPER;
          case NICKEL:
            return CoinColor.NICKEL;
          case DIME: case QUARTER:
            return CoinColor.SILVER;
          default:
            throw new AssertionError("Unknown
    coin: " + c);
        }
    }
}
```

Running the program prints:

```
PENNY:          1¢      COPPER
NICKEL:         5¢      NICKEL
DIME:           10¢     SILVER
QUARTER:        25¢     SILVER
```

In the following example, a playing card class is built atop two simple enum types. Note that each enum type would be as long as the entire example in the absence of the enum facility:

```
import java.util.*;
public class Card implements Comparable<Card>,
    java.io.Serializable {
   public enum Rank { DEUCE, THREE, FOUR, FIVE,
    SIX, SEVEN, EIGHT, NINE, TEN,JACK,
QUEEN, KING, ACE }
   public enum Suit { CLUBS, DIAMONDS, HEARTS,
    SPADES }
    private final Rank rank;
    private final Suit suit;
    private Card(Rank rank, Suit suit) {
        if (rank == null || suit == null)
           throw new NullPointerException(rank
```

```
+ ", " + suit);
        this.rank = rank;
        this.suit = suit;
    }
    public Rank rank() { return rank; }
    public Suit suit() { return suit; }
   public String toString() { return rank + "
   of " + suit; }
   // Primary sort on suit, secondary sort on
   rank
   public int compareTo(Card c) {
                       int suitCompare =
   suit.compareTo(c.suit);
      return (suitCompare != 0 ? suitCompare
   : rank.compareTo(c.rank));
   }
      private static final List<Card>
   prototypeDeck = new ArrayList<Card>(52);
   static {
       for (Suit suit : Suit.values())
           for (Rank rank : Rank.values())
                       prototypeDeck.add(new
   Card(rank, suit));
   }
   // Returns a new deck
   public static List<Card> newDeck() {
                           return new
   ArrayList<Card>(prototypeDeck);
   }
}
```

Here's a little program that exercises the **Card** class. It takes two integer parametres on the command line, representing the number of hands to deal and the number of cards in each hand:

```
import java.util.*;
class Deal {
    public static void main(String args[]) {
        int numHands =
    Integer.parseInt(args[0]);
```

```
        int cardsPerHand =
Integer.parseInt(args[1]);
        List<Card> deck  = Card.newDeck();
        Collections.shuffle(deck);
        for (int i=0; i < numHands; i++)
            System.out.println(dealHand(deck,
cardsPerHand));
    }
    /**
     * Returns a new ArrayList consisting of
the last n elements of
     * deck, which are removed from deck.  The
returned list is
     * sorted using the elements' natural
ordering.
    */
     public static <E extends Comparable<E>>
ArrayList<E>
          dealHand(List<E> deck, int n) {
        int deckSize = deck.size();
                    List<E>   handView   =
deck.subList(deckSize - n, deckSize);
              ArrayList<E>  hand  =  new
ArrayList<E>(handView);
        handView.clear();
        Collections.sort(hand);
        return hand;
    }
}
```

```
Running the program produces results like this:
java Deal 4 5
[FOUR of SPADES, NINE of CLUBS, NINE of SPADES,
    QUEEN of SPADES, KING of SPADES]
[THREE of DIAMONDS, FIVE of HEARTS, SIX of
    SPADES, SEVEN of DIAMONDS, KING of
DIAMONDS]
[FOUR of DIAMONDS, FIVE of SPADES, JACK of
    CLUBS, ACE of DIAMONDS, ACE of
```

```
HEARTS]
[THREE of HEARTS, FIVE of DIAMONDS, TEN of
    HEARTS, JACK of HEARTS, QUEEN of HEARTS]
```

The next example demonstrates the use of constant-specific class bodies to attach behaviours to the constants. (It is anticipated that the need for this will be rare.):

```
import java.util.*;
public enum Operation {
    PLUS {
      double eval(double x, double y) { return
    x + y; }
    },
    MINUS {
      double eval(double x, double y) { return
    x - y; }
    },
    TIMES {
      double eval(double x, double y) { return
    x * y; }
    },
    DIVIDED_BY {
      double eval(double x, double y) { return
    x / y; }
    };
      // Perform the arithmetic operation
    represented by this constant
    // abstract double eval(double x, double
    y);
    public static void main(String args[]) {
      double x = Double.parseDouble(args[0]);
      double y = Double.parseDouble(args[1]);

      for (Operation op : Operation.values())
          System.out.println(x + " " + op +
    " " + y + " = " + op.eval(x, y));
    }
}
```

Running this program produces the following

```
    output:
java Operation 2.0 4.0
2.0 PLUS 4.0 = 6.0
2.0 MINUS 4.0 = -2.0
2.0 TIMES 4.0 = 8.0
2.0 DIVIDED_BY 4.0 = 0.5
```

The above pattern is suitable for moderately sophisticated programmers. It is admittedly a bit tricky, but it is much safer than using a case statement in the base type (Operation), as the pattern precludes the possibility of forgetting to add a behaviour for a new constant (you'd get a compile-time error).

6

Arrays

INTRODUCTION

In the Java programming language *arrays* are objects, are dynamically created, and may be assigned to variables of type `Object`.All methods of class `Object` may be invoked on an array. An array object contains a number of variables. The number of variables may be zero, in which case the array is said to be *empty*.

The variables contained in an array have no names; instead they are referenced by array access expressions that use nonnegative integer index values. These variables are called the *components* of the array. If an array has *n* components, we say *n* is the *length* of the array; the components of the array are referenced using integer indices from 0 to *n*-1, inclusive.

All the components of an array have the same type, called the *component type* of the array. If the component type of an array is *T*, then the type of the array itself is written *T*[]. The value of an array component of type `float` is always an element of the float value set; similarly, the value of an array component of type `double` is always an element of the double value set.

It is not permitted for the value of an array component of type `float` to be an element of the float-extended-exponent value set that is not also an element of the float value set, nor for the value of an array component of type `double` to be an element of the double-extended-exponent value set that is not also an element of the double value set. The component type of an array may itself be an array type. The components of such an array may contain references to subarrays. If, starting from any array type, one considers its component type, and then (if that is also an array type) the component type of that type, and so on, eventually one must reach a component type that is not an array type; this is called the *element type* of the original array, and the components at this level of the data structure are called the *elements* of the original array.

There are some situations in which an element of an array can be an array: if the element type is `Object` or `Cloneable` or `java.io.Serializable`, then some or all of the elements may be arrays, because any array object can be assigned to any variable of these types.

ARRAY TYPES

An array type is written as the name of an element type followed by some number of empty pairs of square brackets `[]`. The number of bracket pairs indicates the depth of array nesting. An array's length is not part of its type.

The element type of an array may be any type, whether primitive or reference. In particular:

- Arrays with an interface type as the component type are allowed. The elements of such an array may have as their value a null reference or instances of any type that implements the interface.
- Arrays with an abstract class type as the component type are allowed. The elements of such an array may have as their value a null reference or instances of any subclass of the abstract class that is not itself abstract.

Array types are used in declarations and in cast expressions.

ARRAY VARIABLES

A variable of array type holds a reference to an object. Declaring a variable of array type does not create an array object or allocate any space for array components. It creates only the variable itself, which can contain a reference to an array. However, the initializer part of a declarator may create an array, a reference to which then becomes the initial value of the variable.

Because an array's length is not part of its type, a single variable of array type may contain references to arrays of different lengths.

Here are examples of declarations of array variables that do not create arrays:

```
int[] ai;         // array of int
short[][] as;     // array of array of short
Object[] ao,      // array of Object
otherAo;          // array of Object
Collection<?>[] ca; // array of Collection of
    unknown type
short s,          // scalar short
aas[][];          // array of array of short
Here are some examples of declarations of array
    variables that create array objects:
Exception ae[]  = new Exception[3];
Object aao[][]  = new Exception[2][3];
int[] factorial = { 1, 1, 2, 6, 24, 120, 720,
    5040 };
char ac[] = { 'n', 'o', 't', ' ', 'a', ' ',
    'S', 't', 'r', 'i', 'n', 'g' };
String[] aas = { "array", "of", "String", };
```

The [] may appear as part of the type at the beginning of the declaration, or as part of the declarator for a particular variable, or both, as in this example:

```
byte[] rowvector, colvector, matrix[];
```

This declaration is equivalent to:

```
byte rowvector[], colvector[], matrix[][];
```

Once an array object is created, its length never changes. To make an array variable refer to an array of different length, a reference to a different array must be assigned to the variable.

If an array variable *v* has type *A*[], where *A* is a reference type, then *v* can hold a reference to an instance of any array type *B*[], provided *B* can be assigned to *A*. This may result in a run-time exception on a assignment.

ARRAY CREATION

An array is created by an array creation expression or an array initializer. An array creation expression specifies the element type, the number of levels of nested arrays, and the length of the array for at least one of the levels of nesting. The array's length is available as a final instance variable **`length`**. It is a compile-time error if the element type is not a reifiable type. An array initializer creates an array and provides initial values for all its components.

ARRAY ACCESS

A component of an array is accessed by an array access expression that consists of an expression whose value is an array reference followed by an indexing expression enclosed by `[` and `]`, as in `A[i]`. All arrays are `0`-origin. An array with length *n* can be indexed by the integers `0` to *n*-1.

Arrays must be indexed by **`int`** values; **`short`**, **`byte`**, or **`char`** values may also be used as index values because they are subjected to unary numeric promotion and become **`int`** values. An attempt to access an array component with a **`long`** index value results in a compile-time error.

All array accesses are checked at run time; an attempt to use an index that is less than zero or greater than or equal to the length of the array causes an `ArrayIndexOutOf BoundsException` to be thrown.

ARRAYS: A SIMPLE EXAMPLE

The example:

```
class Gauss {
    public static void main(String[] args) {
        int[] ia = new int[101];
        for (int i = 0; i < ia.length; i++)
            ia[i] = i;
        int sum = 0;
        for (int e : ia)
            sum += e;
        System.out.println(sum);
    }
```

```
}
that produces the output:
5050
```

declares a variable **ia** that has type array of **int**, that is, **int[]**. The variable **ia** is initialized to reference a newly created array object, created by an array creation expression.The array creation expression specifies that the array should have **101** components. The length of the array is available using the field **length**, as shown.

The example program fills the array with the integers from 0 to 100, sums these integers, and prints the result.

ARRAY INITIALIZERS

An *array initializer* may be specified in a declaration, or as part of an array creation expression, creating an array and providing some initial values:

```
ArrayInitializer:
    { VariableInitializersopt ,opt }
VariableInitializers:
    VariableInitializer
    VariableInitializers , VariableInitializer
The following is repeated from to make the
    presentation here clearer:
VariableInitializer:
    Expression
    ArrayInitializer
```

An array initializer is written as a comma-separated list of expressions, enclosed by braces "{" and "}". The length of the constructed array will equal the number of expressions. The expressions in an array initializer are executed from left to right in the textual order they occur in the source code. The *n*th variable initializer specifies the value of the *n-1*st array component.

Each expression must be assignment-compatible with the array's component type, or a compile-time error results. It is a compile-time error if the component type of the array being initialized is not reifiable. If the component type is itself an array type, then the expression specifying a component may itself be an array initializer; that is, array initializers may be nested. A trailing comma may appear after the last expression in an array initializer and is ignored.

As an example:

```
class Test {
    public static void main(String[] args) {
        int ia[][] = { {1, 2}, null };
        for (int[] ea : ia)
            for (int e: ea)
                System.out.println(e);
    }
}
prints:
1
2
```

before causing a **NullPointerException** in trying to index the second component of the array **ia**, which is a null reference.

ARRAY MEMBERS

The members of an array type are all of the following:

- The public final field length, which contains the number of components of the array (length may be positive or zero).
- The public method clone, which overrides the method of the same name in class Object and throws no checked exceptions. The return type of the clone method of an array type *T[]* is *T[]*.
- All the members inherited from class Object; the only method of Object that is not inherited is its clone method.

An array thus has the same public fields and methods as the following class:

```
class A<T> implements Cloneable,
   java.io.Serializable {
   public final int length = X;
   public T[] clone() {
        try {
        return (T[])super.clone(); //
```

```
    unchecked warning
        } catch (CloneNotSupportedException
    e) {
            throw                          new
    InternalError(e.getMessage());
        }
    }
}
```

Note that the cast in the example above would generate an unchecked warning if arrays were really implemented this way.

Every array implements the interfaces Cloneable and java.io.Serializable.

That arrays are cloneable is shown by the test program:

```
class Test {
    public static void main(String[] args) {
        int ia1[] = { 1, 2 };
        int ia2[] = ia1.clone();
        System.out.print((ia1 == ia2) + " ");
        ia1[1]++;
        System.out.println(ia2[1]);
    }
}
```

which prints:

```
false 2
```

showing that the components of the arrays referenced by `ia1` and `ia2` are different variables. (In some early implementations of the Java programming language this example failed to compile because the compiler incorrectly believed that the clone method for an array could throw a `CloneNotSupportedException`.) A `clone` of a multidimensional array is shallow, which is to say that it creates only a single new array. Subarrays are shared.

This is shown by the example program:

```
class Test {
    public static void main(String[] args)
    throws Throwable {
```

```
        int ia[][] = { { 1 , 2}, null };
        int ja[][] = ia.clone();
        System.out.print((ia == ja) + " ");
        System.out.println(ia[0] == ja[0] &&
    ia[1] == ja[1]);
    }
}
```

which prints:

```
false true
```

showing that the `int[]` array that is `ia[0]` and the `int[]` array that is `ja[0]` are the same array.

CLASS OBJECTS FOR ARRAYS

Every array has an associated `Class` object, shared with all other arrays with the same component type. The direct superclass of an array type is `Object`. Every array type implements the interfaces `Cloneable` and `java.io.Serializable`.

This is shown by the following example code:

```
class Test {
    public static void main(String[] args) {
        int[] ia = new int[3];
        System.out.println(ia.getClass());

    System.out.println(ia.getClass().getSuperclass());
    }
}
```

which prints:

```
class [I
class java.lang.Object
```

where the string "`[I`" is the run-time type signature for the class object "array with component type `int`".

AN ARRAY OF CHARACTERS IS NOT A STRING

In the Java programming language, unlike C, an array of `char` is not a `String`, and neither a `String` nor an array of `char` is terminated by `'\u0000'` (the NUL character). A `String` object is immutable, that is, its contents never change, while an array of **char** has mutable elements. The method **toCharArray** in class **String** returns an array of characters containing the same character sequence as a **String**. The class **StringBuffer** implements useful methods on mutable arrays of characters.

ARRAY STORE EXCEPTION

If an array variable *v* has type *A*[], where *A* is a reference type, then *v* can hold a reference to an instance of any array type *B*[], provided *B* can be assigned to *A*.

Thus, the example:

```
class Point { int x, y; }
class ColoredPoint extends Point { int color;
    }
class Test {
    public static void main(String[] args) {
        ColoredPoint[] cpa = new
    ColoredPoint[10];
        Point[] pa = cpa;
        System.out.println(pa[1] == null);
        try {
            pa[0] = new Point();
        } catch (ArrayStoreException e) {
            System.out.println(e);
        }
    }
}
```

produces the output:

```
true
java.lang.ArrayStoreException
```

Here the variable **pa** has type **Point[]** and the variable **cpa** has as its value a reference to an object of type **ColoredPoint[]**. A **ColoredPoint** can be assigned to a **Point**; therefore, the value of **cpa** can be assigned to **pa**.

A reference to this array **pa**, for example, testing whether **pa[1]** is **null**, will not result in a run-time type error. This is because the element of the array of type **ColoredPoint[]** is a **ColoredPoint**, and every **ColoredPoint** can stand in for a **`Point`**, since **`Point`** is the superclass of **`ColoredPoint`**. On the other hand, an assignment to the array **`pa`** can result in a run-time error. At compile time, an assignment to an element of **`pa`** is checked to make sure that the value assigned is a **`Point`**. But since **`pa`** holds a reference to an array of **`ColoredPoint`**, the assignment is valid only if the type of the value assigned at run-time is, more specifically, a **`ColoredPoint`**.

The Java virtual machine checks for such a situation at run-time to ensure that the assignment is valid; if not, an **`ArrayStoreException`** is thrown. More formally: an assignment to an element of an array whose type is *A*[], where *A* is a reference type, is checked at run-time to ensure that the value assigned can be assigned to the actual element type of the array, where the actual element type may be any reference type that is assignable to *A*.

7

Execution of Program

INTRODUCTION

A Java virtual machine starts up by loading a specified class and then invoking the method **main** in this specified class. Section outlines the loading, linking, and initialization steps involved in executing **main**, as an introduction to the concepts in this chapter. Further sections specify the details of loading, linking, and initialization.

The chapter continues with a specification of the procedures for creation of new class instances; and finalization of class instances. It concludes by describing the unloading of classes and the procedure followed when a program exits.

VIRTUAL MACHINE START-UP

A Java virtual machine starts execution by invoking the method **main** of some specified class, passing it a single argument, which is an array of strings. In the examples in this specification, this first class is typically called **Test**.

The manner in which the initial class is specified to the Java virtual machine is beyond the scope of this specification, but it is typical, in host environments that use command lines, for the fully-qualified name of the class to be specified as a command-line argument and for following command-line arguments to be used as strings to be provided as the argument to the method **main**. For example, in a UNIX implementation, the command line:

```
java Test reboot Bob Dot Enzo
```

will typically start a Java virtual machine by invoking method **main** of class **Test** (a class in an unnamed package), passing it an array containing the four strings `"reboot"`, `"Bob"`, `"Dot"`, and `"Enzo"`.

LOAD THE CLASS TEST

The initial attempt to execute the method **`main`** of class **`Test`** discovers that the class **`Test`** is not loaded-that is, that the virtual machine does not currently contain a binary representation for this class. The virtual machine then uses a class loader to attempt to find such a binary representation. If this process fails, then an error is thrown.

LINK TEST: VERIFY, PREPARE, (OPTIONALLY) RESOLVE

After **`Test`** is loaded, it must be initialized before **`main`** can be invoked. And **`Test`**, like all (class or interface) types, must be linked before it is initialized. Linking involves verification, preparation and (optionally) resolution.

Verification checks that the loaded representation of **`Test`** is well-formed, with a proper symbol table. Verification also checks that the code that implements **`Test`** obeys the semantic requirements of the Java programming language and the Java virtual machine. If a problem is detected during verification, then an error is thrown. Preparation involves allocation of static storage and any data structures that are used internally by the virtual machine, such as method tables. Resolution is the process of checking symbolic references from **`Test`** to other classes and interfaces, by loading the other classes and interfaces that are mentioned and checking that the references are correct. The resolution step is optional at the time of initial linkage. An implementation may resolve symbolic references from a class or interface that is being linked very early, even to the point of resolving all symbolic references from the classes and interfaces that are further referenced, recursively.

(This resolution may result in errors from these further loading and linking steps.) This implementation choice represents one extreme and is similar to the kind of "static" linkage that has been done for many years in simple implementations of the C language. (In these implementations, a compiled program is typically represented as an "`a.out`" file that contains a fully-linked version of the program, including completely resolved links to library routines used by the program. Copies of these library routines are included in the "`a.out`" file.) An implementation may instead choose to resolve a symbolic reference only when it is actively used; consistent use of this strategy for all symbolic references would represent the "laziest" form of resolution. In this case, if `Test` had several symbolic references to another class, then the references might be resolved one at a time, as they are used, or perhaps not at all, if these references were never used during execution of the program.

The only requirement on when resolution is performed is that any errors detected during resolution must be thrown at a point in the program where some action is taken by the program that might, directly or indirectly, require linkage to the class or interface involved in the error. Using the "static" example implementation choice described above, loading and linkage errors could occur before the program is executed if they involved a class or interface mentioned in the class `Test` or any of the further, recursively referenced, classes and interfaces. In a system that implemented the "laziest" resolution, these errors would be thrown only when an incorrect symbolic reference is actively used.

INITIALIZE TEST: EXECUTE INITIALIZERS

In our continuing example, the virtual machine is still trying to execute the method `main` of class `Test`. This is permitted only if the class has been initialized. Initialization consists of execution of any class variable initializers and static initializers of the class `Test`, in textual order. But before `Test` can be initialized, its direct superclass must be initialized, as well as the direct superclass of its direct superclass, and so on, recursively. In the simplest case, `Test` has `Object` as its implicit direct superclass; if class `Object` has not yet been initialized, then it must be initialized before `Test` is initialized. Class `Object` has no superclass, so the recursion terminates here. If class `Test` has another class `Super` as its superclass, then

`Super` must be initialized before `Test`. This requires loading, verifying, and preparing `Super` if this has not already been done and, depending on the implementation, may also involve resolving the symbolic references from `Super` and so on, recursively. Initialization may thus cause loading, linking, and initialization errors, including such errors involving other types.

INVOKE TEST.MAIN

Finally, after completion of the initialization for class `Test` (during which other consequential loading, linking, and initializing may have occurred), the method `main` of `Test` is invoked. The method `main` must be declared `public`, `static`, and `void`. It must accept a single argument that is an array of strings. This method can be declared as either

```
public static void main(String[] args)
or
public static void main(String... args)
```

LOADING OF CLASSES AND INTERFACES

Loading refers to the process of finding the binary form of a class or interface type with a particular name, perhaps by computing it on the fly, but more typically by retrieving a binary representation previously computed from source code by a compiler, and constructing, from that binary form, a `Class` object to represent the class or interface.

Well-behaved class loaders maintain these properties:

- Given the same name, a good class loader should always return the same class object.
- If a class loader *L1* delegates loading of a class *C* to another loader *L2*, then for any type *T* that occurs as the direct superclass or a direct superinterface of *C*, or as the type of a field in *C*, or as the type of a formal parametre of a method or constructor in *C*, or as a return type of a method in *C*, *L1* and *L2* should return the same class object.

A malicious class loader could violate these properties. However, it could not undermine the security of the type system, because the Java virtual machine guards against this. A basic principle of the design of the Java programming language is that the run-time type system cannot be subverted by code written in the language, not even by implementations of such otherwise sensitive system classes as **`ClassLoader`** and **`SecurityManager`**.

THE LOADING PROCESS

The loading process is implemented by the class **`ClassLoader`** and its subclasses. Different subclasses of **`ClassLoader`** may implement different loading policies. In particular, a class loader may cache binary representations of classes and interfaces, prefetch them based on expected usage, or load a group of related classes together. These activities may not be completely transparent to a running application if, for example, a newly compiled version of a class is not found because an older version is cached by a class loader. It is the responsibility of a class loader, however, to reflect loading errors only at points in the program they could have arisen without prefetching or group loading. If an error occurs during class loading, then an instance of one of the following subclasses of class **`LinkageError`** will be thrown at any point in the program that (directly or indirectly) uses the type:

- ClassCircularityError: A class or interface could not be loaded because it would be its own superclass or superinterface.
- ClassFormatError: The binary data that purports to specify a requested compiled class or interface is malformed.
- NoClassDefFoundError: No definition for a requested class or interface could be found by the relevant class loader.

Because loading involves the allocation of new data structures, it may fail with an **`OutOfMemoryError`**.

LINKING OF CLASSES AND INTERFACES

Linking is the process of taking a binary form of a class or interface type and combining it into the runtime state of the

Java virtual machine, so that it can be executed. A class or interface type is always loaded before it is linked. Three different activities are involved in linking: verification, preparation, and resolution of symbolic references. Here we present an overview of the process from the viewpoint of the Java programming language. This specification allows an implementation flexibility as to when linking activities (and, because of recursion, loading) take place, provided that the semantics of the language are respected, that a class or interface is completely verified and prepared before it is initialized, and that errors detected during linkage are thrown at a point in the program where some action is taken by the program that might require linkage to the class or interface involved in the error.

For example, an implementation may choose to resolve each symbolic reference in a class or interface individually, only when it is used (lazy or late resolution), or to resolve them all at once while the class is being verified (static resolution). This means that the resolution process may continue, in some implementations, after a class or interface has been initialized. Because linking involves the allocation of new data structures, it may fail with an `OutOfMemoryError`.

VERIFICATION OF THE BINARY REPRESENTATION

Verification ensures that the binary representation of a class or interface is structurally correct. For example, it checks that every instruction has a valid operation code; that every branch instruction branches to the start of some other instruction, rather than into the middle of an instruction; that every method is provided with a structurally correct signature; and that every instruction obeys the type discipline of the Java virtual machine language.

For the specification of the verification process, see the separate volume of this series, *The Java Virtual Machine Specification*. and the specification of the J2ME Connected Limited Device Configuration, version 1.1. If an error occurs during verification, then an instance of the following subclass of class **LinkageError** will be thrown at the point in the program that caused the class to be verified:

- VerifyError: The binary definition for a class or interface failed to pass a set of required checks to verify that it obeys the semantics of the Java virtual machine language and that it cannot violate the integrity of the Java virtual machine.

PREPARATION OF A CLASS OR INTERFACE TYPE

Preparation involves creating the **static** fields (class variables and constants) for a class or interface and initializing such fields to the default values.This does not require the execution of any source code; explicit initializers for **static** fields are executed as part of initialization, not preparation. Implementations of the Java virtual machine may precompute additional data structures at preparation time in order to make later operations on a class or interface more efficient. One particularly useful data structure is a "method table" or other data structure that allows any method to be invoked on instances of a class without requiring a search of superclasses at invocation time.

RESOLUTION OF SYMBOLIC REFERENCES

The binary representation of a class or interface references other classes and interfaces and their fields, methods, and constructors symbolically, using the binary names of the other classes and interfaces. For fields and methods, these symbolic references include the name of the class or interface type of which the field or method is a member, as well as the name of the field or method itself, together with appropriate type information. Before a symbolic reference can be used it must undergo *resolution*, wherein a symbolic reference is checked to be correct and, typically, replaced with a direct reference that can be more efficiently processed if the reference is used repeatedly. If an error occurs during resolution, then an error will be thrown. Most typically, this will be an instance of one of the following subclasses of the class **IncompatibleClass ChangeError**, but it may also be an instance of some other subclass of **IncompatibleClassChangeError** or even an instance of the class **IncompatibleClassChangeError** itself. This error may be thrown at any point in the program that uses a symbolic reference to the type, directly or indirectly:

- *IllegalAccessError*: A symbolic reference has been encountered that specifies a use or assignment of a field, or invocation of a method, or creation of an instance of a class, to which the code containing the reference does not have access because the field or method was declared private, protected, or default access (not public), or because the class was not declared public.

This can occur, for example, if a field that is originally declared **public** is changed to be **private** after another class that refers to the field has been compiled.

- *InstantiationError*: A symbolic reference has been encountered that is used in class instance creation expression, but an instance cannot be created because the reference turns out to refer to an interface or to an abstract class.

This can occur, for example, if a class that is originally not **abstract** is changed to be **abstract** after another class that refers to the class in question has been compiled.

- *NoSuchFieldError*: A symbolic reference has been encountered that refers to a specific field of a specific class or interface, but the class or interface does not contain a field of that name.

This can occur, for example, if a field declaration was deleted from a class after another class that refers to the field was compiled.

- NoSuchMethodError: A symbolic reference has been encountered that refers to a specific method of a specific class or interface, but the class or interface does not contain a method of that signature.

This can occur, for example, if a method declaration was deleted from a class after another class that refers to the method was compiled. Additionally, an **UnsatisfiedLinkError** (a subclass of **LinkageError**) may be thrown if a class declares a `native` method for which no implementation can be found. The error will occur if the method is used, or earlier, depending on what kind of resolution strategy is being used by the virtual machine.

INITIALIZATION OF CLASSES AND INTERFACES

Initialization of a class consists of executing its static initializers and the initializers for `static` fields (class variables) declared in the class. Initialization of an interface consists of executing the initializers for fields (constants) declared there. Before a class is initialized, its superclass must be initialized, but interfaces implemented by the class are not initialized. Similarly, the superinterfaces of an interface are not initialized before the interface is initialized.

WHEN INITIALIZATION OCCURS

Initialization of a class consists of executing its static initializers and the initializers for static fields declared in the class. *Initialization* of an interface consists of executing the initializers for fields declared in the interface.

Before a class is initialized, its direct superclass must be initialized, but interfaces implemented by the class need not be initialized. Similarly, the superinterfaces of an interface need not be initialized before the interface is initialized.

A class or interface type *T* will be initialized immediately before the first occurrence of any one of the following:

- *T* is a class and an instance of *T* is created.
- *T* is a class and a static method declared by *T* is invoked.
- A static field declared by *T* is assigned.
- A static field declared by *T* is used and the field is not a constant variable.
- *T* is a top-level class, and an assert statement lexically nested within *T* is executed.

Invocation of certain reflective methods in class `Class` and in package `java.lang.reflect` also causes class or interface initialization. A class or interface will not be initialized under any other circumstance. The intent here is that a class or interface type has a set of initializers that put it in a consistent state, and that this state is the first state that is observed by other classes. The static initializers and class variable initializers are executed in textual order, and may not refer to class variables declared in the class whose declarations appear textually after the use, even though these class variables are in scope. This restriction is designed to detect, at compile time, most circular or otherwise malformed initializations. As shown in an example in, the fact that initialization code is unrestricted allows examples to be constructed where the value of a class variable can be observed when it still has its initial default value, before its initializing expression is evaluated, but such examples are rare in practice. Such examples can be also constructed for instance variable initialization. The full power of the language is available in these initializers; programmers must exercise some care. This power places an extra burden on code generators, but this burden would arise in any case because the language is concurrent. Before a class is initialized, its superclasses are initialized, if they have not previously been initialized.

Thus, the test program:

```
class Super {
    static { System.out.print("Super "); }
}
class One {
    static { System.out.print("One "); }
}
class Two extends Super {
    static { System.out.print("Two "); }
}
class Test {
    public static void main(String[] args) {
          One o = null;
          Two t = new Two();
          System.out.println((Object)o ==
    (Object)t);
    }
```

```
}
prints:
Super Two false
```

The class `One` is never initialized, because it not used actively and therefore is never linked to. The class `Two` is initialized only after its superclass `Super` has been initialized. A reference to a class field causes initialization of only the class or interface that actually declares it, even though it might be referred to through the name of a subclass, a subinterface, or a class that implements an interface.

The test program:

```
class Super { static int taxi = 1729; }
class Sub extends Super {
    static { System.out.print("Sub "); }
}
class Test {
    public static void main(String[] args) {
        System.out.println(Sub.taxi);
    }
}
prints only:
1729
```

because the class `Sub` is never initialized; the reference to `Sub.taxi` is a reference to a field actually declared in class `Super` and does not trigger initialization of the class `Sub`. Initialization of an interface does not, of itself, cause initialization of any of its superinterfaces.

Thus, the test program:

```
interface I {
    int i = 1, ii = Test.out("ii", 2);
}
interface J extends I {
    int j = Test.out("j", 3), jj = Test.out("jj",
    4);
}
interface K extends J {
    int k = Test.out("k", 5);
}
```

```
class Test {
    public static void main(String[] args) {
        System.out.println(J.i);
        System.out.println(K.j);
    }
    static int out(String s, int i) {
        System.out.println(s + "=" + i);
        return i;
    }
}
produces the output:
1
j=3
jj=4
3
```

The reference to `J.i` is to a field that is a compile-time constant; therefore, it does not cause `I` to be initialized. The reference to `K.j` is a reference to a field actually declared in interface `J` that is not a compile-time constant; this causes initialization of the fields of interface `J`, but not those of its superinterface `I`, nor those of interface `K`. Despite the fact that the name `K` is used to refer to field `j` of interface `J`, interface `K` is not initialized.

DETAILED INITIALIZATION PROCEDURE

Because the Java programming language is multithreaded, initialization of a class or interface requires careful synchronization, since some other thread may be trying to initialize the same class or interface at the same time. There is also the possibility that initialization of a class or interface may be requested recursively as part of the initialization of that class or interface; for example, a variable initializer in class *A* might invoke a method of an unrelated class *B*, which might in turn invoke a method of class *A*.

The implementation of the Java virtual machine is responsible for taking care of synchronization and recursive initialization by using the following procedure. It assumes that the `Class` object has already been verified and prepared, and that the `Class` object contains state that indicates one of four situations:

- This Class object is verified and prepared but not initialized.
- This Class object is being initialized by some particular thread *T*.
- This Class object is fully initialized and ready for use.
- This Class object is in an erroneous state, perhaps because initialization was attempted and failed.

The procedure for initializing a class or interface is then as follows:

1. Synchronize on the Class object that represents the class or interface to be initialized. This involves waiting until the current thread can obtain the lock for that object.
2. If initialization is in progress for the class or interface by some other thread, then wait on this Class object (which temporarily releases the lock). When the current thread awakens from the wait, repeat this step.
3. If initialization is in progress for the class or interface by the current thread, then this must be a recursive request for initialization. Release the lock on the Class object and complete normally.
4. If the class or interface has already been initialized, then no further action is required. Release the lock on the Class object and complete normally.
5. If the Class object is in an erroneous state, then initialization is not possible. Release the lock on the Class object and throw a NoClassDefFoundError.
6. Otherwise, record the fact that initialization of the Class object is now in progress by the current thread and release the lock on the Class object.
7. Next, if the Class object represents a class rather than an interface, and the superclass of this class has not yet been initialized, then recursively perform this entire procedure for the superclass. If necessary, verify and prepare the superclass first. If the initialization of the superclass completes abruptly

because of a thrown exception, then lock this Class object, label it erroneous, notify all waiting threads, release the lock, and complete abruptly, throwing the same exception that resulted from initializing the superclass.

8. Next, determine whether assertions are enabled for this class by querying its defining class loader.
9. Next, execute either the class variable initializers and static initializers of the class, or the field initializers of the interface, in textual order, as though they were a single block, except that final class variables and fields of interfaces whose values are compile-time constants are initialized first.
10. If the execution of the initializers completes normally, then lock this Class object, label it fully initialized, notify all waiting threads, release the lock, and complete this procedure normally.
11. Otherwise, the initializers must have completed abruptly by throwing some exception *E*. If the class of *E* is not Error or one of its subclasses, then create a new instance of the class Exception In Initializer Error, with *E* as the argument, and use this object in place of *E* in the following step. But if a new instance of Exception InInitializer Error cannot be created because an Out Of Memory Error occurs, then instead use an OutOfMemoryError object in place of *E* in the following step.
12. Lock the Class object, label it erroneous, notify all waiting threads, release the lock, and complete this procedure abruptly with reason *E* or its replacement as determined in the previous step.

IMPLICATIONS FOR CODE GENERATION

Code generators need to preserve the points of possible initialization of a class or interface, inserting an invocation of the initialization procedure just described. If this initialization procedure completes normally and the `Class` object is fully initialized and ready for use, then the invocation of the initialization procedure is no longer necessary and it may be eliminated from the code-for example, by patching it out or otherwise regenerating the code.

Compile-time analysis may, in some cases, be able to eliminate many of the checks that a type has been initialized from the generated code, if an initialization order for a group of related types can be determined. Such analysis must, however, fully account for concurrency and for the fact that initialization code is unrestricted.

CREATION OF NEW CLASS INSTANCES

A new class instance is explicitly created when evaluation of a class instance creation expression causes a class to be instantiated.

A new class instance may be implicitly created in the following situations:

- Loading of a class or interface that contains a String literal may create a new String object to represent that literal. (This might not occur if the same String has previously been interned.
- Execution of an operation that causes boxing conversion. Boxing conversion may create a new object of a wrapper class associated with one of the primitive types.
- Execution of a string concatenation operator that is not part of a constant expression sometimes creates a new String object to represent the result. String concatenation operators may also create temporary wrapper objects for a value of a primitive type.

Each of these situations identifies a particular constructor to be called with specified arguments as part of the class instance creation process. Whenever a new class instance is created, memory space is allocated for it with room for all the instance variables declared in the class type and all the instance variables declared in each superclass of the class type, including all the instance variables that may be hidden. If there is not sufficient space available to allocate memory for the object, then creation of the class instance completes abruptly with an

`OutOfMemoryError`. Otherwise, all the instance variables in the new object, including those declared in superclasses, are initialized to their default values. Just before a reference to the newly created object is returned as the result, the indicated constructor is processed to initialize the new object using the following procedure:

1. Assign the arguments for the constructor to newly created parametre variables for this constructor invocation.
2. If this constructor begins with an explicit constructor invocation of another constructor in the same class, then evaluate the arguments and process that constructor invocation recursively using these same five steps. If that constructor invocation completes abruptly, then this procedure completes abruptly for the same reason; otherwise, continue with step 5.
3. This constructor does not begin with an explicit constructor invocation of another constructor in the same class (using this). If this constructor is for a class other than Object, then this constructor will begin with an explicit or implicit invocation of a superclass constructor (using super). Evaluate the arguments and process that superclass constructor invocation recursively using these same five steps. If that constructor invocation completes abruptly, then this procedure completes abruptly for the same reason. Otherwise, continue with step 4.
4. Execute the instance initializers and instance variable initializers for this class, assigning the values of instance variable initializers to the corresponding instance variables, in the left-to-right order in which they appear textually in the source code for the class. If execution of any of these initializers results in an exception, then no further initializers are processed and this procedure completes abruptly with that same exception. Otherwise, continue with step 5. (In some early implementations, the compiler incorrectly omitted the code to initialize a field if the field

initializer expression was a constant expression whose value was equal to the default initialization value for its type.)

5. Execute the rest of the body of this constructor. If that execution completes abruptly, then this procedure completes abruptly for the same reason. Otherwise, this procedure completes normally.

In the example:

```
class Point {
    int x, y;
    Point() { x = 1; y = 1; }
}
class ColoredPoint extends Point {
    int color = 0xFF00FF;
}
class Test {
    public static void main(String[] args) {
  ColoredPoint cp = new ColoredPoint();
            System.out.println(cp.color);
        }
}
```

A new instance of `ColoredPoint` is created. First, space is allocated for the new `ColoredPoint`, to hold the fields `x`, `y`, and `color`. All these fields are then initialized to their default values (in this case, `0` for each field). Next, the `ColoredPoint` constructor with no arguments is first invoked. Since `ColoredPoint` declares no constructors, a default constructor of the form:

```
ColoredPoint() { super(); }
```

is provided for it automatically by the Java compiler.

This constructor then invokes the `Point` constructor with no arguments. The `Point` constructor does not begin with an invocation of a constructor, so the compiler provides an implicit invocation of its superclass constructor of no arguments, as though it had been written:

```
Point() { super(); x = 1; y = 1; }
```

Therefore, the constructor for `Object` which takes no arguments is invoked. The class `Object` has no superclass, so the recursion terminates here. Next, any instance initializers, instance variable initializers of `Object` are invoked. Next, the body of the constructor of `Object` that takes no arguments is executed. No such constructor is declared in `Object`, so the compiler supplies a default one, which in this special case is:

```
Object() { }
```

This constructor executes without effect and returns. Next, all initializers for the instance variables of class `Point` are executed. As it happens, the declarations of `x` and `y` do not provide any initialization expressions, so no action is required for this step of the example.

Then the body of the `Point` constructor is executed, setting `x` to `1` and `y` to `1`. Next, the initializers for the instance variables of class `ColoredPoint` are executed. This step assigns the value `0xFF00FF` to `color`.

Finally, the rest of the body of the `ColoredPoint` constructor is executed (the part after the invocation of `super`); there happen to be no statements in the rest of the body, so no further action is required and initialization is complete. Unlike C++, the Java programming language does not specify altered rules for method dispatch during the creation of a new class instance.

If methods are invoked that are overridden in subclasses in the object being initialized, then these overriding methods are used, even before the new object is completely initialized. Thus, compiling and running the example:

```
class Super {
    Super() { printThree(); }
          void printThree() {
    System.out.println("three"); }
}
class Test extends Super {
    int three = (int)Math.PI;
    // That is, 3
    public static void main(String[] args) {
          Test t = new Test();
          t.printThree();
    }
```

```
        void printThree() {
    System.out.println(three);  }
}
produces the output:
0
3
```

This shows that the invocation of printThree in the constructor for class Super does not invoke the definition of printThree in class Super, but rather invokes the overriding definition of printThree in class Test. This method therefore runs before the field initializers of Test have been executed, which is why the first value output is 0, the default value to which the field three of Test is initialized.

The later invocation of printThree in method main invokes the same definition of printThree, but by that point the initializer for instance variable three has been executed, and so the value 3 is printed.

FINALIZATION OF CLASS INSTANCES

The class `Object` has a **`protected`** method called **`finalize`**; this method can be overridden by other classes. The particular definition of **`finalize`** that can be invoked for an object is called the *finalizer* of that object. Before the storage for an object is reclaimed by the garbage collector, the Java virtual machine will invoke the finalizer of that object. Finalizers provide a chance to free up resources that cannot be freed automatically by an automatic storage manager. In such situations, simply reclaiming the memory used by an object would not guarantee that the resources it held would be reclaimed.

The Java programming language does not specify how soon a finalizer will be invoked, except to say that it will happen before the storage for the object is reused. Also, the language does not specify which thread will invoke the finalizer for any given object. It is guaranteed, however, that the thread that invokes the finalizer will not be holding any user-visible synchronization locks when the finalizer is invoked. If an uncaught exception is thrown during the finalization, the exception is ignored and finalization of that object terminates. The completion of an object's constructor happens-before the execution of its **finalize** method (in the formal sense of happens-before). Discussion: It is important to note that many finalizer threads may be active (this is sometimes needed on large shared memory multiprocessors), and that if a large connected data structure becomes garbage, all of the finalize methods for every object in that data structure could be invoked at the same time, each finalizer invocation running in a different thread. The **finalize** method declared in class **Object** takes no action. The fact that class **Object** declares a **finalize** method means that the **finalize** method for any class can always invoke the **finalize** method for its superclass. This should always be done, unless it is the programmer's intent to nullify the actions of the finalizer in the superclass.

(Unlike constructors, finalizers do not automatically invoke the finalizer for the superclass; such an invocation must be coded explicitly.) For efficiency, an implementation may keep track of classes that do not override the **finalize** method of class **Object**, or override it in a trivial way, such as:

```
   protected void finalize() throws Throwable
{
   super.finalize();
   }
```

We encourage implementations to treat such objects as having a finalizer that is not overridden, and to finalize them more efficiently. A finalizer may be invoked explicitly, just like any other method.

The package **java.lang.ref** describes weak references, which interact with garbage collection and finalization. As with any API that has special interactions with the language, implementors must be cognizant of any requirements imposed by the **java.lang.ref** API. This specification does not discuss weak references in any way. Readers are referred to the API documentation for details.

IMPLEMENTING FINALIZATION

Every object can be characterized by two attributes: it may

be *reachable, finalizer-reachable,* or *unreachable,* and it may also be *unfinalized, finalizable,* or *finalized.* A *reachable* object is any object that can be accessed in any potential continuing computation from any live thread. Optimizing transformations of a program can be designed that reduce the number of objects that are reachable to be less than those which would naively be considered reachable. For example, a compiler or code generator may choose to set a variable or parametre that will no longer be used to **null** to cause the storage for such an object to be potentially reclaimable sooner.

Discussion: Another example of this occurs if the values in an object's fields are stored in registers. The program may then access the registers instead of the object, and never access the object again. This would imply that the object is garbage. Note that this sort of optimization is only allowed if references are on the stack, not stored in the heap.

For example, consider the *Finalizer Guardian* pattern:

```
class Foo {
    private final Object finalizerGuardian =
    new Object() {
    protected void finalize() throws Throwable
    {
        /* finalize outer Foo object */
      }
    }
  }
```

The finalizer guardian forces super.finalize to be called if a subclass overrides finalize and does not explicitly call super.finalize. If these optimizations are allowed for references that are stored on the heap, then the compiler can detect that the finalizerGuardian field is never read, null it out, collect the object immediately, and call the finalizer early.

This runs counter to the intent: the programmer probably wanted to call the Foo finalizer when the Foo instance became unreachable. This sort of transformation is therefore not legal: the inner class object should be reachable for as long as the outer class object is reachable. Transformations of this sort may result in invocations of the finalize method occurring earlier than might be otherwise expected. In order to allow the user to prevent this, we enforce the notion that synchronization may keep the object alive. *If an object's finalizer can result in synchronization on that object, then that object must be alive and considered reachable whenever a lock is held on it.*

Note that this does not prevent synchronization elimination: synchronization only keeps an object alive if a finalizer might synchronize on it. Since the finalizer occurs in another thread, in many cases the synchronization could not be removed anyway.

A *finalizer-reachable* object can be reached from some finalizable object through some chain of references, but not from any live thread. An *unreachable* object cannot be reached by either means.

An *unfinalized* object has never had its finalizer automatically invoked; a *finalized* object has had its finalizer automatically invoked. A *finalizable* object has never had its finalizer automatically invoked, but the Java virtual machine may eventually automatically invoke its finalizer.

An object *o* is not finalizable until its constructor has invoked the constructor for `Object` on *o* and that invocation has completed successfully (that is, without throwing an exception). Every pre-finalization write to a field of an object must be visible to the finalization of that object. Furthermore, none of the pre-finalization reads of fields of that object may see writes that occur after finalization of that object is initiated.

Interaction with the Memory Model

It must be possible for the memory model to decide when it can commit actions that take place in a finalizer. This section describes the interaction of finalization with the memory model.

Each execution has a number of *reachability decision points,* labeled *di*. Each action either *comes-before di* or *comes-after di*. Other than as explicitly mentioned, the comes-before ordering described in this section is unrelated to all other orderings in the memory model. If *r* is a read that sees a write *w* and *r* comes-before *di*, then *w* must come-before *di*. If *x* and *y* are synchronization actions on the same variable or monitor such that *so(x, y)* and *y* comes-before *di*, then *x* must come-before *di*. At each reachability decision point, some set of objects are marked as unreachable, and some subset of those objects are marked as finalizable. These reachability decision points are also the points at which references are checked, enqueued and cleared according to the rules provided in the API documentation for the package **`java.lang.ref`**.

The only objects that are considered definitely reachable at a point *di* are those that can be shown to be reachable by the application of these rules:

- An object *B* is definitely reachable at *di* from static fields if there exists a write *w1* to a static field *v* of a class *C* such that the value written by *w1* is a reference to *B*, the class *C* is loaded by a reachable classloader and there does not exist a write *w2* to *v* such that *hb(w2, w1)* is not true and both *w1* and *w2* come-before *di*.
- An object *B* is definitely reachable from *A* at *di* if there is a write *w1* to an element *v* of *A* such that the value written by *w1* is a reference to *B* and there does not exist a write *w2* to *v* such that *hb(w2, w1)* is not true and both *w1* and *w2* come-before *di*.
- If an object *C* is definitely reachable from an object *B*, and object *B* is definitely reachable from an object *A*, then C is definitely reachable from *A*.

An action *a* is an active use of X if and only if at least one of the following conditions holds:

- *A* reads or writes an element of X
- *A* locks or unlocks X and there is a lock action on X that happens-after the invocation of the finalizer for X.
- *A* writes a reference to X
- *A* is an active use of an object *Y*, and X is definitely reachable from *Y*

If an object X is marked as unreachable at *di*,

- X must not be definitely reachable at *di* from static fields,

- All active uses of *X* in thread *t* that come-after *di* must occur in the finalizer invocation for X or as a result of thread *t* performing a read that comes-after *di* of a reference to X.
- All reads that come-after *di* that see a reference to X must see writes to elements of objects that were unreachable at *di*, or see writes that came after *di*.

If an object *X* is marked as finalizable at *di*, then

- *X* must be marked as unreachable at *di*,
- *di* must be the only place where *X* is marked as finalizable,
- Actions that happen-after the finalizer invocation must come-after *di*

FINALIZER INVOCATIONS ARE NOT ORDERED

The Java programming language imposes no ordering on finalize method calls. Finalizers may be called in any order, or even concurrently. As an example, if a circularly linked group of unfinalized objects becomes unreachable (or finalizer-reachable), then all the objects may become finalizable together. Eventually, the finalizers for these objects may be invoked, in any order, or even concurrently using multiple threads. If the automatic storage manager later finds that the objects are unreachable, then their storage can be reclaimed. It is straightforward to implement a class that will cause a set of finalizer-like methods to be invoked in a specified order for a set of objects when all the objects become unreachable. Defining such a class is left as an exercise for the reader.

UNLOADING OF CLASSES AND INTERFACES

An implementation of the Java programming language may *unload* classes. A class or interface may be unloaded if and only if its defining class loader may be reclaimed by the garbage collector. Classes and interfaces loaded by the bootstrap loader may not be unloaded. *Here is the rationale for the rule given in the previous paragraph*: Class unloading is an optimization that helps reduce memory use. Obviously, the semantics of a program should not depend on whether and how a system chooses to implement an optimization such as class unloading. To do otherwise would compromise the portability of programs. Consequently, whether a class or interface has been unloaded or not should be transparent to a program. However, if a class or interface C was unloaded while its defining loader was potentially reachable, then C might be reloaded. One could never ensure that this would not happen. Even if the class was not referenced by any other currently loaded class, it might be referenced by some class or interface, *D*, that had not yet been loaded. When *D* is loaded by *C*'s defining loader, its execution might cause reloading of C.

Reloading may not be transparent if, for example, the class has:

- Static variables (whose state would be lost).
- Static initializers (which may have side effects).
- Native methods (which may retain static state).

Furthermore the hash value of the `Class` object is dependent on its identity. Therefore it is, in general, impossible to reload a class or interface in a completely transparent manner. Since we can never guarantee that unloading a class or interface whose loader is potentially reachable will not cause reloading, and reloading is never transparent, but unloading must be transparent, it follows that one must not unload a class or interface while its loader is potentially reachable. A similar line of reasoning can be used to deduce that classes and interfaces loaded by the bootstrap loader can never be unloaded.

One must also argue why it is safe to unload a class C if its defining class loader can be reclaimed. If the defining loader can be reclaimed, then there can never be any live references to it. This, in turn, can only be true if there are can never be any live references to any of the classes defined by that loader, including C, either from their instances or from code. Class unloading is an optimization that is only significant for applications that load large numbers of classes and that stop using most of those classes after some time. A prime example of such an application is a web browser, but there are others. A characteristic of such applications is that they manage classes through explicit use of class loaders. As a result, the policy outlined above works well for them.

Bibliography

Abrahams, L.: *Proposal to Add Contract Programming to C++,* New York: McGraw–Hill, *2003.*

Bruce, Hendrickson and Robert, Leland*: Algorithms and Software for Partitioning Meshes,* New Jersey: Engelwood Cliffs, 2000.

Coplien, James O.: *Advanced C++, Programming Styles and Idioms,* UK: Addison Wesley Publishing Company, 2002.

David, G.: *Linear and Nonlinear Programming,* UK: Addison–Wesley Publishing Company, 2004.

Dennis, J. E.: *Quasi-newton Methods, Motivation and Theory,* UK: SIAM Review, 2001.

Enseling, O.: *Contract Programming for Java,* New York: McGraw–Hill, 2003.

Fletcher, R.: *Practical Methods of Optimization,* India: John Wiley and Sons, 2002.

Henricson, Mats: *Programming in C++, Rules and Recomendations,* Sweden: Ellemtel Telecomunication Systems Laboratories, 2003.

Herbert, S.: *The Emerging Network Marketplace,* New Jersey: Ablex Publishing, 2000.

Joshi, Mahesh: *Object-Oriented Programming, Systems, Languages and Applications*. Minnesota: Univesity of Minnesota and IBM , 2002.

Kevin, Dowd: *High Performance Computing,* Morris Street: O' Reilly and Associates, 2005.

Kumar, Sumit: *Multilevel Algorithms for Multi–constraint Graph Partitioning,* Minnesota: Univesity of Minnesota and Army HPC Research Centre, 2002.

McConnell, J.: *Internetworking Computer Systems : Interconnecting Networks and Systems,* New Jersey: Prentice Hall, 2001.

Olton, Mark: *Beowulf Class Parallel Computer "GeoWulf": Design, Construction and Testing,* California: University of California, 2007.

Stallings, W.: *Handbook of Computer-Communications Standards,* New York: Macmillan, 2003.

Stoll, C.: *The Cuckoo's Egg: Tracking a Spy through the Maze of Computer Espionage,* New York: Doubleday, 1999.

Stroustrup, B.: *The C++ Programming Language,* Hertfordshire: Prentice Hall, 2001.

Tanenbaum, A.: *Computer Networks,* New Jersey: Prentice Hall, 1999.

Vallee, J.: *The Network Revolution,* California: Press, Berkeley, 2005.

Index

F

G

H

I

J

L

M

N

O

P

S

T

U